Plough Quarterly

BREAKING GROUND FOR A RENEWED WORLD

Summer 2017, Number 13

Artists: Bruce Herman, Jason Landsel, Jane Chapin, Graham Berry, Fra Angelico, Francisco de Zurbarán, Eleanor Fortescue-Brickdale, Matthew J. Cutter, John August Swanson, Vittorio Matteo Corcos, Leon Dabo

Cover: Paweł Kuczyński. See portfolio on page 53.

WWW.PLOUGH.COM

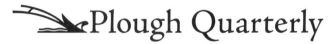

Plough Quarterly

WWW.PLOUGH.COM

Meet the community behind *Plough*.

Plough Quarterly is published by the Bruderhof, an international community of families and singles seeking to follow Jesus together. Members of the Bruderhof are committed to a way of radical discipleship in the spirit of the Sermon on the Mount. Inspired by the first church in Jerusalem (Acts 2 and 4), they renounce private property and share everything in common in a life of nonviolence, justice, and service to neighbors near and far.

The community includes families and single people from a wide range of backgrounds, with around 2,700 people in all. There are twenty-three Bruderhof settlements in both rural and urban locations in the United States, England, Germany, Australia, and Paraguay.

To learn more or arrange a visit, see the community's website at *bruderhof.com*.

Plough Quarterly features original stories, ideas, and culture to inspire everyday faith and action. Starting from the conviction that the teachings and example of Jesus can transform and renew our world, we aim to apply them to all aspects of life, seeking common ground with all people of goodwill regardless of creed. The goal of *Plough Quarterly* is to build a living network of readers, contributors, and practitioners so that, in the words of Hebrews, we may "spur one another on toward love and good deeds."

Plough Quarterly includes contributions that we believe are worthy of our readers' consideration, whether or not we fully agree with them. Views expressed by contributors are their own and do not necessarily reflect the editorial position of *Plough* or of the Bruderhof communities.

Editors: Peter Mommsen, Sam Hine, Maureen Swinger. Art director: Emily Alexander. Online editor: Erna Albertz.
Contributing editors: Susannah Black, Shana Burleson.
Founding Editor: Eberhard Arnold (1883–1935).
Plough Quarterly No. 13: Save Our Souls
Published by Plough Publishing House, ISBN 978-0-87486-177-8
Copyright © 2017 by Plough Publishing House. All rights reserved.

Scripture quotations (unless otherwise noted) are from the New Revised Standard Version Bible, copyright © 1989 the Division of Christian Education of the National Council of the Churches of Christ in the United States of America. Used by permission. All rights reserved. Front cover and page 3: Paweł Kuczyński, *Sharks I* and *Sharks II*. Used by permission. Inside front cover: © Jane Chapin, *Afternoon at the Jerome*. Used by permission. Back cover: Graham Berry, *Early Morning Fishing*. Used by permission.

Editorial Office	Subscriber Services	United Kingdom	Australia
PO Box 398	PO Box 345	Brightling Road	4188 Gwydir Highway
Walden, NY 12586	Congers, NY 10920-0345	Robertsbridge	Elsmore, NSW
T: 845.572.3455	T: 800.521.8011	TN32 5DR	2360 Australia
info@plough.com	*subscriptions@plough.com*	T: +44(0)1580.883.344	T: +61(0)2.6723.2213

Plough Quarterly (ISSN 2372-2584) is published quarterly by Plough Publishing House, PO Box 398, Walden, NY 12586.
Individual subscription $32 per year in the United States; Canada add $8, other countries add $16.
Periodicals postage paid at Walden, NY 12586 and at additional mailing offices.
POSTMASTER: Send address changes to *Plough Quarterly*, PO Box 345, Congers, NY 10920-0345.

Reality to the Rescue

Dear Reader,

How much of your day – how much of my day – is spent in reality, and how much in a fake world? Eons ago, when Steve Jobs was still young, cyber-utopians promised that technology would soon end tyranny and usher in a new age of peace, egalitarianism, rainbows, and butterflies. Few today still credit such prophecies. Four decades into the techno-logical age, we've learned that screen time is bad for you, too much media consumption damages your heart, and Facebook can make you mentally ill. We all know this. But what are we to do about it?

"We have retreated into a simplified and often completely fake version of the world. But because it is all around us, we accept it as normal." That's how Adam Curtis introduces his remarkable 2016 BBC documentary *HyperNormalisation*. He compares the fake world in which most Westerners spend their waking hours to the bubble of falsity in which Soviet citizens lived in the 1970s – they knew the Communist regime was crumbling, but were so invested in it that they pretended its lies were true. "You were so much a part of the system," the film explains, "that you were unable to see beyond it."

Today's "system" isn't just technology, dramatically as that has changed our lives. Nor is it some sinister conspiracy of the global

Davoisie. It's a fakeness we hardly register anymore: the mind-altering power of the advertising that invades virtually every corner of our lives; the dehumanizing us-versus-them passions of our polarized politics; the fact that millions of us have learned to multitask while watching footage of refugees drowning. As Paweł Kuczyński's satirical art vividly illustrates (page 53), this fake world is invading our souls.

So it's in our souls that we must find the cure. The stakes are high. Our inner life will never remain a vacuum for long – Jesus tells us that when one demon is driven out, seven new ones stand ready to take its place. If we allow ourselves to be distracted, or passively accept the fake realities of our age, we are lost.

Sound alarmist? Eberhard Arnold, the German thinker who started *Plough* a century ago and whose writings inspired this issue, saw twice in his lifetime how a loss of inner integrity can have terrifyingly real results for entire nations. The first time was in World War I, when German Christians rushed to support the Kaiser's war-crazed nationalism, resulting in millions of deaths. The second was in the 1930s, when these same fellow Christians (with honorable but rare exceptions) embraced Nazism. How was it possible, Arnold wondered, that even the most pious believers were sucked into these satanic depravities?

Only a return to inwardness, Arnold believed, could bring distracted moderns back to Jesus and to constructive work for his kingdom. Inwardness, he writes, echoing Kierkegaard, involves cleansing our soul and conscience, concentrating our will on what is of eternal value, and silencing our own opinions and desires so that we can hear the promptings of God's spirit (page 18).

Activist types may object at this point that focusing on "inwardness" is all very well – no doubt a few spiritual disciplines are healthy, just like jogging or yoga – but surely in a world where a thousand tragedies cry out for our time and resources, isn't it the height of selfishness to retreat into our interior life? Shouldn't we rather be out saving starving children, not narcissistically squandering our energies on the spiritual equivalent of body building?

Is inwardness just the spiritual equivalent of body building?

No, answers Arnold forcefully, because inwardness is the opposite of self-worship. Nothing, after all, is more agonizing to the ego than the inward work of the Holy Spirit. And the goal of the Spirit's work is nothing less than the coming of God's kingdom on earth. That's why Christians through the ages have insisted that inwardness is crucial to the life of discipleship. Jesus himself retreated to the wilderness for forty days at the start of his ministry and returned to the desert at other pivotal moments of his life. As Meister Eckhart, the early Quakers, and Cardinal Sarah teach us (pages 20, 31, and 32), the key to hearing God is inner detachment and silence. "When inwardness is missing," writes Kierkegaard, "the spirit is made finite. Inwardness is the eternal."

This encounter with the eternal is what keeps us from falling for demagogues and false gospels, whether on the left or the right. It saves us from a life wasted on superficialities, and from ignoring our neighbor.

Inwardness, then, is the soil in which human community and active service must be rooted if they are to bear good fruit. This is hardly a new idea: throughout Christian history it was often the mystics who were most active in serving others, as we see in the examples of the medieval Beguines and of Simone Weil (page 25), in awkward saints such as Gerard Manley Hopkins (page 60), and in the pugnacious faith of Fannie Lou Hamer (page 80). Today, the same truth shines out from witnesses such as Paolo Dall'Oglio, Frans van der Lugt, and Jacques Mourad, three priests in Syria whom Stephanie Saldaña remembers on page 44.

It shines out, too, in another life that we remember in these pages: that of Johann Christoph Arnold, the Bruderhof elder and *Plough* author who died on Holy Saturday this year. In our lead article, his son Heinrich brings out the essence – and some colorful details – of his father's life and legacy (page 8).

These lives give us a glimpse of the real world from which our fake world seeks to distract us. It's a bracing, even painful, vision at times; as T. S. Eliot remarked, "humankind cannot bear very much reality." Yet such reality – the superabundant life of the kingdom of God – is what Jesus will bring in fullness when he comes again. Until then, to adapt the words of Paul, we must refuse to be conformed to the fake world. May this issue serve to help us in this, so that we can love in deed and in truth.

Warm greetings,

Peter

Peter Mommsen, *Editor*

Learning to Be Human

On Maureen Swinger's "The Teacher Who Never Spoke," Spring 2017:

My oldest stepson, Chris, is an adult with a diagnosis of Lennox-Gastaut Syndrome. It's pretty rare, which is why I was taken by surprise this week when I read this terrific story. Chris is a teacher, too. He is the happiest, most loving person I've ever known. He not only teaches his siblings about the joys of simplicity, but he also teaches our eight grandchildren what love, acceptance, and even joy look like.

From their earliest days, our grandchildren have spent time around Chris and come to understand his likes, his limits, his love. They begin to grasp that Chris is far from the only person around with special needs, which means this is all part of normal human life. And they begin to recognize that while having Chris may mean extra work for his family and other caregivers, it also means learning that each person is of inestimable value, no matter what that person's limits. Join me in standing against the crushing philosophy of utilitarianism.

Bill Tammeus, Kansas City, MO

The New Testament is peppered with the paradox of up and down, great and small, first and last: "If anyone would be first, he must be last of all, and servant of all" (Mark 9:35). This is one of those stories that illustrates that paradox, and it's one of the reasons why this story is my favorite of the latest issue.

Julius McCarter, Loudon, TN

I was especially touched by this piece, as my dance studio is located inside a facility that serves people who are abled differently. I teach creative movement to some of the daytime participants and have become humbled by learning patience and a more flexible teaching style that then is extended toward my afternoon students studying classical ballet. This piece reminded me how often the teacher–student role has been reversed in my letting go of how I think things ought to be – and at those moments, grace rolls in.

Diana Turner-Forte, Ellerbe, NC

Vittorio Matteo Corcos, *Dreams*

How to Not Burn Out

On D. L. Mayfield's "Confronted by Dorothy," Spring 2017:

You rightly say that Dorothy Day showed immense perseverance in her work for social justice and "gave herself daily in unspectacular acts of love." I wrote to her from England in 1973 asking if I could come and help in her New York house of hospitality. She apologized in her reply, saying that she was in Fresno County Jail in California for supporting the United Farm Workers led by César Chavez, but she "would ready me a bed" when she got out. While with her in the New York house, I asked how she had managed to run the soup kitchen, offer a home to so many people, produce a newspaper, take part in demonstrations, etc., for the last forty years. I was expecting a pious answer; instead she said, "Two days off a week!" She went on to say that without that break for recreation (i.e., to re-create yourself with cultural pursuits), you would burn out and be unable to carry on the work. From my short time there I found Dorothy very wise, full of common sense, and with a great sense of humor.

Peter Keeling, Middlesbrough, UK

Thank you so much for your candor and your courage. I'm deeply touched and hope to garner strength for another day in our troubled world. I also hope to pay it forward in my daily life, my "work." A deep bow to you from a Buddhist in St. Louis.

Keith Roper, St. Louis, MO

Wendell Berry Responds

On Tamara Hill Murphy's "The Hole in Wendell Berry's Gospel," Winter 2017:
Tamara Hill Murphy makes much of my technological heresy: "He . . . writes books without a computer, farms . . . without a tractor." I must hurry to add: Though I believe those choices to be entirely defensible ecologically and economically, and therefore religiously and politically, I have never recommended them to particular persons or to the public. A pencil and a team of horses are dangerous when used without skill and experience, and perhaps even more dangerous when used without pleasure.

More important, Ms. Murphy's article involves a geographic and economic misconception that your readers ought to consider. She assumes that my writing is necessarily false if it does not confirm, or is not confirmed by, her family's experience "in the center of New York State," or the experience of J. D. Vance's family "in rural Kentucky" and in "a Rust Belt town in . . . Ohio," which Mr. Vance recounts in his book, *Hillbilly Elegy.*

I have no authoritative knowledge about the center of New York State. And about a Rust Belt town in Ohio I know principally what I have learned from Mr. Vance's book. About Kentucky I have perhaps a fair amount of genuine knowledge that I have gotten from experience, observation, and reading. Ms. Murphy's error is in her assumption that "rural Kentucky" is one homogenous place. In fact, Kentucky is a state of several regions, and my region is in a number of ways unlike Mr. Vance's.

Mr. Vance's family's homeland is Breathitt County in eastern Kentucky, a region that, for more than a century, has been dominated by the one-product economy of coal. The social and ecological impact of that economy on that region has been devastating.

My home county of Henry, about two hundred miles northwest of Breathitt County, has been blessed by its paucity of mineable minerals. For about sixty years of my own lifetime, largely because of the federal tobacco program, this economy was also agrarian. The land was divided fairly democratically, and there were a lot of small farms on which families and neighbors worked together. My county, nevertheless, since the end of World War II, has been increasingly affected by the influence, the values, the enterprises, and the products of the industrial economy, which is now entirely dominant. That dominance has brought to us the dislocation, disintegration, aimlessness, drug addiction, and other evils that Mr. Vance writes about.

But in his book, like Ms. Murphy in her article, Mr. Vance does not look at the colonialist predation inherent in industrialism, or at the difference between the industrial economy that would preserve and employ kindly the land and the people of every region. That is a difference well worth thinking about.

Wendell Berry, Port Royal, KY

We welcome letters to the editor. Letters and web comments may be edited for length and clarity, and may be published in any medium. Letter should be sent with the writer's name and address to letters@plough.com. ⤳

City and Kingdom New York

New Yorkers can be countercultural too! The newly launched City and Kingdom New York network seeks to explore the theological and practical aspects of living truly countercultural lives as New Yorkers. Meetings will highlight different ways that locals are living out the dual citizenship of Christian discipleship: seeking the good of the city while owing final allegiance to the New Jerusalem. To receive information about upcoming events, or to explore City and Kingdom for your own hometown, sign up at *plough.com/cityandkingdom*.

Bruderhof for a Day

Interested in experiencing Christianity as a way of life, not a religion? Join us at Fox Hill, a Bruderhof community in Walden, New York, on the first Saturday of every month for a day of work, fun, and conversation.

The Bruderhof, the community that publishes *Plough,* seeks to respond to Jesus' demanding call in the Sermon on the Mount by following the communal traditions of the early church. "Love your neighbor, share everything" – at this fraught historical moment, the practical faith of the early Christians seems like an especially compelling answer to the problems of contemporary society.

Bruderhof for a Day is an immersive opportunity to experience a very different way of life and draw inspiration to find and pursue your own calling. Dave, a construction worker who participated, said his visit "was a good reminder that God's call on our lives is all-encompassing, and [it] challenged me to live out my kingdom calling more explicitly. Christ's kingdom includes my workplace and my town."

Allison, a fashion marketer who has not been a practicing Christian, said that "spending

Planting broccoli at a "Bruderhof for a Day" event at Fox Hill community

time with a community suffused with faith was striking and exciting. I believe that part of what we owe for the gift of life is to keep our minds and hearts open to others and to what they can teach us, always being ready to . . . reassess our default assumptions. . . . The day was a chance to practice that belief. I went home and cracked open a Bible for the first time in many years."

Rone, a businessman who has been drawn to intentional community, said that his visit "allowed this vision to come to life and provoked me to invest my time, energy, and income [in] the broken world around me more than ever. I look forward to coming again!" Sign up at *bruderhof.com/foraday*.

Poet in This Issue: Malcolm Guite

Malcolm Guite is a poet, priest, the chaplain of Girton College in Cambridge, England, and lead singer for the band Mystery Train. He is the author of eight books, including *What Do Christians Believe?* and *Sounding the Seasons.* His poems "A Lens" and "Ordinary Saints" appear on pages 36 and 43. ➤

Malcolm Guite, poet, singer, and guitarist, fronts the blues-rock band Mystery Train.

J. HEINRICH ARNOLD II

Not a Saint, but a Prophet

Remembering My Father, Johann Christoph Arnold

RIFTON, NEW YORK, APRIL 19, 2017, "Now I know the meaning of what it truly is to 'rest in peace.'" A tear traced the old man's history-weathered face as he embraced my brother and me. Smiling, he added, "This is peace." My father had died three days before, and Dr. John Perkins, the civil rights hero and founder of the Christian Community Development Association, had come from Mississippi to pay tribute to his old friend and fellow peacemaker. We were gathered around my father's body, facing the mystery of eternal life. To rest in peace is a reward for work in life.

My father, Johann Christoph Arnold, was many things: a pastor, an elder in the Bruderhof, a veteran of the fight for peace and reconciliation through forgiveness, a warrior in the struggle to live the gospel and love his neighbor.

His wake reflected this life's work. People streamed into the room: families from the Bruderhof with small children in tow, older people pushed in wheelchairs, lifelong coworkers from the clergy, and hundreds of students. Neighbors he'd visited were there, alongside contractors and plumbers, doctors and nurses,

8

politicians and droves of men and women in law enforcement and emergency services. In the middle of it all, Cardinal Timothy Dolan swept in to offer embraces, a heartfelt prayer for the deceased, and humorous recollections of his and my father's shared work for the Lord – and their shared love of German sausage and beer.

How do you draw the essence of a man who lived by inspiration and the Holy Spirit? Right about here, Dad would cut me off with, "I'm not a saint! Don't paint me as a saint." True, with his walking stick in hand and his straight-shooting manner, Dad was more prophet-like than saintly. He was a pillar: constant, trustworthy, unfaltering, unafraid of wind and weather. A life like his, lived in primal faith in Christ, is at once too simple and too profound to explain. To capture it is to kill it: it is lived, and its intensity burns an image preserved as legend. It's a hard portrait to paint, and I am no painter. But I can scratch hieroglyphics.

Origins

In 1936, Johann Heinrich Arnold and his wife, Annemarie Hedwig Wächter, fled from Nazi oppression in Germany to Britain, where Dad was born in 1940, the third of nine children. (My great-grandfather, Eberhard Arnold, had founded the Bruderhof in 1920 along with my great-grandmother Emmy and her sister Else von Hollander.)

Soon enough, my grandparents and their children had to leave England, along with the rest of the Bruderhof. Germans were considered enemy aliens. They crossed the U-boat-infested Atlantic by ship and settled in the jungles of Paraguay, where the community carved out a living by farming and handcrafts. Dad was shaped by the perseverance and toughness required in this pioneering childhood. Underlying his upbringing was the Fifth Commandment: "Honor your father and your mother, as the Lord your God has commanded you, so that you may live long and that it may go well with you in the land the Lord your God is giving you" (Deut. 5:16). I realize now, after hearing Dad repeat these words more times than I could count, that his obedience to this commandment underpinned his legacy and blessed his accomplishments.

Becoming American

In 1955, the family moved with the Bruderhof to the United States. His infectious smile, sunny nature, and love for people propelled my father through the challenges of learning a new language and culture.

Kingston High School class of 1959

He loved the America he met at Kingston High School in upstate New York. He ran track, got a dish-washing job, and met Elvis before the singer was too famous to perform in small-town venues. His English teacher instilled in him a lifelong love of Shakespeare, so that sixty years later he would unexpectedly recite passages from *Macbeth* or *Hamlet*.

He stood out among his peers with his strong German accent – and his refusal to recite the Pledge of Allegiance. As the son of refugees who had fled Hitler, he had absorbed a deep suspicion of uncritical loyalty to state power. Yet he was enormously proud to become an American, precisely because freedom of conscience was enshrined in the Constitution. It was this freedom that he exercised when,

J. Heinrich Arnold II is a physician's assistant, schoolteacher, and pastor. He lives with his family at Woodcrest, a Bruderhof community in upstate New York.

around this time, he made his own commitment to the Bruderhof.

Charting the Course

Johann Christoph Arnold at the funeral of Jimmie Lee Jackson, 1965

In early 1965, my father, having recently earned a business degree, was working as a freshly minted salesman for Community Playthings, the Bruderhof's toy manufacturing business. On a business trip to Atlanta, he flicked on the old motel television set to the breaking news that a young black man, Jimmie Lee Jackson, had just died in Selma, Alabama, after being shot eight days earlier at a peaceful voting rights march.

Dad was drawn to the civil rights movement like a magnet. His father had stood up for justice and peace during the Second World War. Was this his moment? He immediately drove the two hundred miles to Selma. What he experienced there is best described in his own words from his book *Why Forgive?*:

> The viewing was open-casket, and although the mortician had done his best to cover the injuries, the wounds on Jimmie's head could not be hidden. The room was packed with about three thousand people. We sat on a windowsill at the back. We never heard one note of anger or revenge in the service. Instead, a spirit of courage emanated from the men and women of the congregation, especially as they rose to sing the old slave song, "Ain't Gonna Let Nobody Turn Me 'Round."
>
> Afterwards, at the cemetery, Martin Luther King spoke about forgiveness and love. He pleaded with his people to pray for the police, to forgive the murderer, and to forgive those who were persecuting them. Then we held hands and sang "We Shall Overcome." . . . If

there was ever cause for hatred or vengeance, it was here. But none was to be felt, not even from Jimmie's parents.

This event transformed my father's life. On that day, he was inspired by a vision that would shape his life and mission until his last breath. His vision was deep and broad, and, like King's, it was often misunderstood. It was not a call to divisive social activism. The cause worth dying for was the kingdom of God coming on earth. Baptism by water and Spirit had sealed his commitment to this kingdom; now he was called to live it out. Love to all, peace, and forgiveness were weapons of power, tools for the courageous believer, not the soft or faint-hearted.

Young Father

Just one year later, in 1966, Dad married Verena Donata Meier. Young and madly in love, they started a family. My seven siblings and I were born within ten years. As busy as life would get, Dad always made time for us. He loved life. He loved practical jokes. He loved the New York Yankees. He loved dogs, and after a childhood with a mutt named Tell, Dad raised nine German Shepherds over sixty years.

Then there was his insatiable love of the outdoors. Hard work splitting and hauling firewood or carting compost was rewarded by swimming in the nearby pond, hiking in the Catskills, fishing the Wallkill, and hunting – activities we kids learned to love as well through his contagious enthusiasm. He loved music, too, especially classical music – Bach, Beethoven, Mendelssohn – and all of us kids learned instruments. Few evenings ended without our family gathering to sing folk songs, hymns, or spirituals, often with neighbor families invited.

In 1972, my father was asked to be a pastor in the Bruderhof. His own father had also been called to pastor, and in 1962 he had been appointed by the members of the Bruderhof as the community's elder. But Dad was enjoying his job in publishing; becoming a pastor was neither his idea nor his wish. Still, the community recognized his God-given pastoral gift – a gift no doubt honed by hours spent with his father as he assisted him in counseling congregants. He and my mother agreed to take up this new task.

Dad could connect with almost anyone he met. He listened more than he spoke, and rather than concrete advice, he would often offer a humorous quip and words of understanding and hope. He was the tireless head coach in a game with no sidelines – everybody was an eligible receiver, and if you were in sight, you were part of the team.

Church Leader

Difficult years came. His mother, with whom he was extremely close, died of cancer in 1980. His father died two years later. The Bruderhof struggled with the loss of its elder and with painful divisions.

The courage and humility needed for forgiveness was put to the test in those years. But forgiveness won out – remarkably, the opposing factions reconciled, and Dad was appointed as the Bruderhof's elder in 1983. Together with his wife, Verena, he bore the responsibility with energy and enthusiasm. He was not all soft: Dad could speak straight and to the point. He

With long-time friend and brother Larry Mason, a Vietnam veteran

was not evasive if he sensed that selfishness was derailing a believer. But, the first to call someone out, he was also the first to forgive, disarming with his warmth and trust. This love that speaks truth, that helps others through repentance to restoration, is where my father did his greatest work. He was blind to social status. Elderly people, military veterans, business executives, ex-felons, addicts, the emotionally fragile, ambitious college grads, politicians, children with disabilities, rebellious teenagers: no matter who you were, Dad would hear you out and prove a trustworthy guide. He was accessible day and night; often his first phone calls and emails were before 5:00 a.m. and the last after 11:00 p.m. If somebody was dying, he and often my mother were at the bedside – dozens of times.

Even as his friends multiplied with each passing year, Dad did make some enemies. Never afraid of controversy, he would say what he meant. By the same token, though, he respected people who held differences of opinion. Two years ago, for instance, he invited our state senator, a friend, to explain to a meeting of our church his support of New York State's recently passed Marriage Equality Act. A heated discussion ensued between the politician

Sex, God, and Marriage

(1996)

Mother Teresa *from the foreword:* "In this book we find a message needed today in every part of the world. To be pure, to remain pure, can only come at a price, the price of knowing God and of loving him enough to do his will."

Pope Benedict XVI: "I am very happy for this book and for its moral conviction."

Why Forgive?

(1997)

Foreword by **Steven McDonald**

Nelson Mandela: "A much-needed message not only for South Africa, but for the whole world."

Seeking Peace

Notes and Conversations along the Way

(1998)

Thich Nhat Hanh *from the preface:* "As you read this book, root out the violence in your life, and learn to live compassionately and mindfully. Seek peace. When you have peace within, real peace with others will be possible."

Cries from the Heart

Stories of Struggle and Hope

(1999)

Robert Coles *from the foreword:* "An unusually telling witness to the power of answered yearning, it will call you to a reawakening of the mind and heart."

and members of our congregation, who defended traditional marriage. When the debate reached an impasse, Dad came to the rescue: "Enough talk. Let's pass around some ice cream and celebrate life and the fact that we can have this exchange with our brother from Albany." We might not have agreed, but we could respect each other and acknowledge our shared goodwill and humanity.

Difference of opinion was one thing, but if someone had an agenda of antagonism, my father would not back down. He had his haters. He didn't relish them, but he used to muse that he could thank them for giving him reassurance in light of Jesus' words: "Woe unto you, when all men shall speak well of you!" (Luke 6:26). Inevitably, he also made his mistakes, as he would be the first to tell you – and at times he became a lightning rod for criticism for his daring decisions and for his sometimes too-generous trust of others.

With a penchant for spontaneity and boldness, my father helped launch a host of new ventures after his appointment as elder. In the late 1980s and early 1990s, he led a surge of joint projects between the Bruderhof and the Hutterite church, continuing a relationship that dated back to 1930. Unfortunately in 1994 this came to an end, largely over his insistence that church leaders, no less than anyone else, must be open to repentance and renewal, which can be the only basis for church unity. This rupture pained him to the end of his life.

Meanwhile, the Bruderhof grew from four communities in two countries to twenty-four communities on four continents; starting in the early 2000s, he encouraged the founding of small urban communities. With his enthusiastic support, the community began fielding rapid-response teams to bring resources to disaster areas and also developed new businesses as sources of revenue. Dad – with Mom always by his side – spoke widely and listened even more widely, trusting those he worked with in ways that encouraged them to contribute far more than they had thought possible.

Proclaiming the Gospel

In 1996, my father published his first book. Eleven more would follow, built on a lifelong love of writing. He found his voice by telling true stories, using them to illustrate his topics: forgiveness, marriage, raising children, education, prayer, fear, hope, death, aging, and finding peace.

For Dad, writing was a collaborative experience. He would ply his congregation for stories, insights, and anecdotes connected to the topic he was writing on, partly for material, but more specifically to engage and broaden our perspectives. His voluminous yellow legal

pads were crowded with longhand thoughts and notes. Dad assembled a solid team, but he was always firmly in charge, involved in every detail of the process. To serve as editor for one of his books was a monumental challenge, but it was rewarded by Dad's humility, enthusiasm, and openness to suggestions and changes.

These books touched many, but *Why Forgive?* is the one that's been most widely read. Its message of forgiveness aims most directly at the heart of the gospel, and it has changed lives.

World travel had always been a part of life for my parents: it was among the responsibilities of being the elder of an international church. Dad cherished these opportunities to learn about people's needs, joys, and sorrows, and always marveled at how similar people are underneath.

With the publication of his books, my father began to receive requests to speak at religious and peacemaking conferences in the United States and across the world. Beginning in the mid-nineties, my parents undertook trips to Israel, Palestine, Iraq, Cuba, South Africa, Mexico, and Rwanda. At the same time, the Bruderhof brought humanitarian aid and the message of the gospel to disaster-ridden or war-torn regions. My father went on many of these missions as well, traveling to Haiti, Thailand, Central America, South America, Africa, and the Middle East. It was in the context of this work, in 1996, that he met Mother Teresa. "She pleaded," he wrote, "that we become involved with the poorest of the poor, and that is where we will find Jesus. If anyone has been an example of how to serve the poorest of the poor, it is she and the Sisters of Charity."

Although his heart was with the poor, Dad didn't forgo opportunities to meet those in high places, including leaders of both good and ill repute. In Iraq he visited and prayed with Saddam Hussein's foreign minister, Tariq Aziz, who was a Christian. In Cuba he

conversed with Fidel Castro, stressing the importance of religious freedom. At the time of the Lewinsky scandal, Dad sent President Clinton a copy of his book on forgiveness, along with a letter; they

Be Not Afraid
Overcoming the Fear of Death
(2000)

Madeleine L'Engle *from the foreword:* "Until we can admit the fear, we cannot know the assurance, deep down in our hearts, that indeed, we are not afraid."

Paul Brand: "I want a copy beside my bed when my time comes."

Escape Routes
For People Who Feel Trapped in Life's Hells
(2002)

Ari Goldman: "Arnold does not give us a magic formula for coping with life's hells – there is none – but gently reminds us that the first step begins with ourselves."

Rich in Years
Finding Peace and Purpose in a Long Life
(2013)

Foreword by **Cardinal Seán O'Malley**

Eugene H. Peterson: "A symphony of voices of men and women willing to talk about aging. There is much beauty here and not a trace of sentimentality."

Their Name Is Today
Reclaiming Childhood in a Hostile World
(2014)

Mark K. Shriver *from the foreword:* "I've already shared my dog-eared manuscript with several friends."

With Cardinal Ratzinger, later Pope Benedict XVI, in Italy (1995), an encounter that marked growing friendships with the Catholic Church

began to correspond about repentance, forgiveness, and the call to live a transformed life. In his autobiography, Clinton acknowledges the importance of this exchange.

Dad called everyone who would listen to the love of God and neighbor that is common to many faiths. Still, though he recognized the image of God in everyone, he was never ashamed to speak of the love of Jesus.

During the decades of his leadership, the Bruderhof made common cause with many workers for peace and justice, from Cesar Chavez of the United Farm Workers Union to Franklin Graham of Samaritan's Purse to Mark Shriver of Save the Children. He worked with Chuck Colson on prison ministry and with Sister Helen Prejean and others on death penalty abolition. In 1995 he struck up a friendship with New York's Cardinal O'Connor, and began to work more closely with his Catholic brothers and sisters, demonstrating his conviction in the power of the gospel to overcome historical divisions. He dialogued with Cardinal Joseph Ratzinger, who would become Pope Benedict XVI, on marriage and family; this relationship led to a 2004 meeting with Pope John Paul II.

It was during this time, too, that Dad made a new connection that would lead to some of the most crucial work of his later years. In 1997, he heard about Detective Steven McDonald, a NYPD cop who had been shot and paralyzed while investigating a rash of crimes in Central Park. Steven had publicly forgiven the fifteen-year-old boy who shot him, and reached out to him while he was incarcerated. Intrigued, Dad arranged a visit to Steven's home on Long Island. After Dad listened to Steven's story, they talked about the power of faith and forgiveness and began to plan ways to

work together to reach troubled youth.

This partnership led to action. They went first to Northern Ireland in 1999, where they met with recently warring Catholics and Protestants. A trip to Israel and Palestine followed, where they spoke at the Knesset and at the Israeli Defense Force headquarters in Jerusalem. In both places they heard many stories of conflict, hatred, and violence, but many, too, of reconciliation and forgiveness.

Soon, the experience that Dad and Steven had gained abroad was needed at home. The shooting at Columbine High School in April of 1999 heralded a growing trend of school violence. Dad and Steven decided to bring the message of forgiveness into schools. Their Breaking the Cycle program has touched thousands. It has brought together a variety of speakers – reformed gang members, the mother of a suicide victim, survivors of alcoholic and drug-addicted households – all with powerful testimonies. Breaking the Cycle's mission – to offer hope and healing through the message of forgiveness, and to model constructive choices – became one of Dad's passions, into which he poured countless hours.

Golden Years

Always forward-thinking, it was at the height of his activity, in 2001, that Dad passed on the eldership of the Bruderhof to Richard Scott. This allowed him to guide the development of the community's leadership and freed him to focus on new forms of outreach – often surprising ones.

Many may wonder why a peace-loving Anabaptist pastor would become a police chaplain. Twenty-five years ago, Dad might have asked the same question. But entering a new field of mission at age sixty-two was typical of his big heart and open mind. His acquaintance with Detective McDonald helped him understand that members of law enforcement have one of the most difficult jobs – to be peacemakers as well as peacekeepers – and that they need support and prayers.

As chaplain to the Ulster County Sheriff's Office and the Ulster County Police Chiefs Association, Dad spoke and prayed with those who needed help processing difficult experiences, visited sick family members, held funerals, and blessed marriages and babies. He delighted in organizing precinct barbecues, a gastronomical liturgy without much preaching. But he did not neglect prayer. On one late-night call to the local emergency room where a young deputy was being attended after a fatal car crash, the undersheriff escorted Dad through a sea of grim, uniformed personnel to pray at the side of this dying young man. The officer later described the scene: "It was like Moses parting the waters; he strode in there with such calm authority and love, bringing reassurance and peace."

His work as a chaplain to officers of the law was not at odds with his decades-long commitment to prison ministry. In whatever company he found himself, he drew on a seemingly limitless reservoir of empathy – a lesson he had learned from Dostoyevsky, another

of his literary lodestars. I'll never forget the night I brought Dad into the county jail at the summons of another prison chaplain to visit a distraught inmate who had been arrested for the heinous rape and murder of a child. He spoke no words of false comfort, nor did he downplay the horror of the crimes committed. But he pointed to Jesus, who could forgive even the worst criminal. The man admitted to the crime, was convicted and given a life sentence, and years later, after confessing his sins, received baptism while in state penitentiary. To this day, the prisoner treasures Dad's personal Bible, a book my father gave him that fateful night, and uses it to minister to fellow prisoners.

After heart surgery in 2006, health problems took their toll on the pace of Dad's activities,

With Steven McDonald and inmates in the Ulster County Jail, 2010

With friend and coworker John Perkins, joined by grandchildren

Walking
stick in hand:
visiting a
friend in the
Paraguayan
leper colony
where his
father worked
in the 1940s

but not on the quickness of his mind and spirit. Dad and Mom were increasingly inseparable as their years of complementarity mounted. The loss of their daughter, Margrit, to cancer – and a long battle with the same ugly disease in my mother – tested our family.

In November 2014, my parents traveled to Rome at the invitation of the Vatican to speak alongside Pope Francis and a host of religious leaders and scholars at the Humanum Colloquium, an international interreligious conference on the sanctity of marriage. Hundreds gathered from all over the world, representing many faiths. Dad spoke:

> Faithful marriage is one of the most wonderful ways one can serve humankind. But marriage is more than a private contract. Marriage is part of God's original creation and sanctifies each generation as being "made in the image of God." Like the early church, we need to become more courageous – a counterculture of simplicity and practical help. . . . The first Christians turned the Roman world upside down partly because husbands and wives remained faithful to one another and to their children. With God's help, we too can do the same today.

Final Battle

The final battlefield was his own cancer, diagnosed this past March. Dad carried on. In between very short rests, he spent time with people who wanted counsel, visited others suffering from illness, and held assemblies at Bruderhof schools. Most afternoons would include a drive into the Hudson Valley countryside to check on fields, woods, and wildlife or to stop at a local restaurant for a cappuccino. But the most significant times were the church gatherings in the evenings. Be simple in faith, he told us, and love each other. Look at life through the eyes of Jesus. Free your hearts from sin by repentance and confession. Forgive, holding no grudges.

He honestly confessed his own fear of death, too, pointing to the gospel as the only remedy. Trust in Jesus and prayer are the weapons, he said, that are required throughout all of life, and none of us outgrows the need of them.

On Palm Sunday, just six days before he died, Dad spoke to our community:

> The main thing is that God's kingdom advances, and if any one of us had the chance

SAVE 55%

SPECIAL O

to play a little part in it, it's not because we are great or mighty, but because God is merciful and he's granting us the possibility to show love.

This past Good Friday, I know Dad was thinking of his Savior's Passion, his suffering. Dad couldn't speak much. He was looking beyond our reality most of the time, but he did say goodbye, with clear, warm eyes and a smile. I asked him for wisdom about the future – of the Bruderhof, of our family, of my own life. "Stay true," he simply said. Dad marched the Golgotha road that day, climbing the mountain to be nearer the gate of life: the cross. We were at his side. It was hard, but there was glory in it. Warriors don't quit, don't lie down. As Holy Saturday dawned, Dad slipped into a coma. Hours later, he drew his last breath while Mom held his face with both her hands. His body was at peace, his soul free. His eyes had seen the glory of the coming of the Lord.

Coda

Years earlier, my wife and I accompanied my parents on a trip to trace the roots of our church and family history in Europe. One day, we were climbing the steep slopes of the Dolomites in northern Italy. Here, in the sixteenth century, Anabaptists had flourished; here my grandfather had been born. Dad was feeling the effects of the altitude and terrain. A thoughtful young companion disappeared into a thicket of mountain ash and hacked down a slender but stout walking stick with a natural crook that fit Dad perfectly. From that time on, the stick was a constant companion. Walking was his connection to the earth; he could feel the life and history of whatever ground he was traveling on. For him, it was all holy ground. The stick was a practical symbol of safety, protection, and authority. We leaned on him – as

Blessed are the peacemakers: Dad's funeral, April 20, 2017

father, as elder. But, as he had taught us, we leaned and will continue to lean even more on the Good Shepherd.

At the wake Dad looked like he was taking a short rest to get ready for his next journey, his stick grasped in his hands as always. It was the picture of peace.

Yes, this is peace; this is rest after a life of action. But the first action, the source of all action and hope, is Christ's offer of redemption and forgiveness through his work on the cross. "He that liveth and believeth in me shall never die," Jesus said (John 11:26). My father lived and acted on this belief.

The room fell silent. Two veteran peacemakers were face to face, one seeing this world, one the next. The living warrior, John Perkins, looked up at us and spoke again. "What a joy it has been for me and my family to know your dad and to appreciate his leadership and his great desire to see the body of Christ united against all racial and cultural barriers. It will happen; this next generation will make that happen. I'm grieving with you, but I want this fellowship and this love to go on and on and to get stronger. So continue your love and good work. Continue to reach out to the broken in our world. I think that is what your dad would want us to do together."

We will go on. Yes, Dad, we will stay true. ⇝

EBERHARD ARNOLD

Inwardness
in a
Distracted
Age

Do you wish
to improve the world?

Good.

But first
seek silence of soul.

What is Christianity's answer when civilization is falling apart? As the conflagration that became World War I spread across Europe, a German theologian, Eberhard Arnold, gave his response in the form of a short book. He last reworked his text, from which these selections are taken, in the thirty-four months between Hitler's rise to power in 1933 and his own death in 1935, titling the new book *Innerland: A Guide into the Heart of the Gospel*. German Christians' shocking openness to Nazism resulted, he believed, from a loss of reverence for the life of the soul. The most effective way to resist evil, then, starts with becoming quiet before God. But it doesn't stop there. »»

GOD WANTS TO GIVE our inward life an indestructible harmony that will work outward in mighty melodies of love. The power that comes from gathering our inner energy is a power for taking action. When our individual hearts are gathered in this way, we will join together as a gathered people – a people whose active work makes God's reign manifest as justice, peace, and joy in the Holy Spirit.

Rom. 14:17

This is the life task to which Christ calls us. Yet today we must first rediscover the importance of deepening our inner life in stillness, otherwise our work will become empty and mechanical, leaving our strength for action sapped at the core. Our spiritual life is watered and made fertile by the holy wellsprings of the inward world, but these will dry up if the stillness within us is lost. Like people dying of thirst, today's overburdened souls long for a quickening of their inner life, sensing that without it they will come to ruin.

Ps. 42:2–3

MEISTER ECKHART: ON INNER DETACHMENT

Francisco de Zurbarán,
Agnus Dei

NOTHING MAKES US true men and women but the giving up of our will. The only perfect and true will comes from entering into God's will and being without self-will. For the perfection of our will means being in harmony with the divine will by willing what God wills, and the way he wills it.

At the time when the angel appeared to our dear Mary, nothing that she had done would ever have made her the mother of God; but as soon as she gave up her will, she became mother of the Eternal Word and conceived God in that hour.

Never has God given himself nor will he ever give himself to an alien will. Only where he finds his will does he impart himself and leave himself, with all that he is.

This is the true inner detachment: in it, the spirit stands immovable in the face of everything that befalls it, whether it is good or bad, honor or disgrace or calumny, just as a broad mountain stands immovable in the face of a little breeze.

IF GOD'S WILL SHOULD please you in this way, you would feel just as if you were in heaven, regardless of what happens or does not happen to you. But those who desire something different from God's will get what they deserve:

The inward power that wells up in the silent stillness in which God himself can speak and act brings us from downfall and death to resurrection and life – a life that pushes outward in streams of creative spirit yet never loses itself in the external world. This strength, which we may call "active stillness," leads believers to a task in the world. It's a task that does not allow them to be conformed to the world, but that also never lets them fall inactive.

The distress of our times makes it unthinkable to retreat from society, willfully blind to the urgent work that calls out for our help. Seeking spiritual detachment must not steer us toward inner and outer isolation from our fellow human beings. (In this respect the sayings of the medieval mystic Meister Eckhart, who wrote extensively on the great value of detachment and who in many ways understood the inner life better than anyone, can easily be misleading.) Thankfully, the rapid mechanization of today's global economy no longer permits such pious selfishness. More than in earlier times, we are protected from deceiving ourselves.

they are always in misery and trouble; people do them a great deal of violence and injury, and they suffer in every way.

We deafen God day and night with our words, "Lord, thy will be done." But then when God's will does happen, we are furious and don't like it a bit. When our will becomes God's will, that is certainly good; but how much better it would be if God's will were to become our will.

THERE IS NOTHING a person is able to offer God that is more pleasing to him than this kind of detachment. God cares less for our watching, fasting, or praying than for this detachment. God needs nothing more from us than a quiet heart.

No one must imagine that it is impossible to attain this, for it is God himself who does it. Some may say they do not have it. To this I say that I am sorry. But if you do not desire it, I am still more sorry. If you cannot have it, then do have a longing for it! And if you cannot have the longing, then at least long to have the longing!

Because of this the prophet says, "I long, O Lord, to have a longing for thy righteousness."

That we may desire God in the sense that he may be born in us – may God help us to this! ⮞

Famous as a mystic after his death, in life Meister Eckhart (ca. 1260–1328) was a noted scholar and active administrator, serving as a Dominican provincial and teaching at the University of Paris. Although his writings were long treated as suspect by the official church – Eckhart died while on trial for heresy – they would later influence both Luther and the Anabaptists and have been cited by recent popes.

Selections from *Meister Eckehart spricht*, ed. Otto Karrer (Ars Sacra/Josef Müller, 1926), trans. Nicoline Maas.

All the same, in our outer activity we will feel a loss in vitality and effectiveness whenever the detachment we strive for has not penetrated to the inmost source of our creative energy. When this power, which springs from inner detachment, is at work in human beings, it will gather together a believing people as a living community. The common life of this people will be characterized both by complete surrender and (as a result) by the most dedicated activity. Their love to all humankind will then press outward from solitude to the very ends of the earth – without ever losing its focal point in the gathered fellowship that remains its source of strength.

To a responsible conscience, the only justification for fleeing the confused and hectic whirl of contemporary culture so as to withdraw into the inward self is if doing so will increase our fruitfulness. The goal must be to unite with eternal powers in order to gain a strength of character that is ready to be tested in the stream of the world and is equipped to meet the demands of our day. Our watchword is not "Retreat!" but rather "Gather for the attack!"

Our watchword is not "Retreat!" but rather "Gather for the attack!"

That is why we may never withdraw from the torrent of present-day life into a spiritual selfishness that chills our love in the face of suffering and guilt. Otherwise our inner detachment will have become far more cold-hearted and unjust than the injustice of the world. Unless we help bear the world's distress and guilt, we will fall prey to a lifeless lie: to eternal and temporal death.

Whoever tries to chop life in half, caring only for the inner needs of others but not for their outer distress, will soon find that he has lost his life's inner half as well – the very part he thought he was securing. Such a one has forgotten Jesus Christ, who bore people's outer and inner needs in equal measure, since in his eyes the two are an inseparable whole.

Matt. 9:4–7

We must participate in the life of today's world with an attitude of militant love. But we can do so only if we are ready to respond with every fiber of our being to the demands that will be made on our labor. With every drop of our hearts' blood we are to share in suffering the world's pain, and so join in struggling with all our vigor to overcome this pain. We will discover how to do this in stillness and in silence.

Gal. 6:2

T HE EXPERIENCE of God means strength for action. Love is always expressed in living deeds; to experience God is to experience his power as living love. Liberation from all unjust, loveless, and self-willed activity releases an abundance of powers that overflow in fruitful works of love. We experience the love of God inwardly, but it manifests itself outwardly. The more our faith increases in knowledge, experience, and strength, the more we will be compelled to do the works of love. To experience God is to be overpowered by love.

Eph. 4:13

Today, the aftereffects of the Great War and the current state of society call for the kind of dedication that lives only in Christ – in the heart of the powerful God of Jesus Christ. Only a heart filled with the superior power of God's love will be able to confront the pain and suffering around it. Only in the strength of an omnipotent God will we be able to carry the burden of historical responsibility laid on us, a burden beyond all human strength. The reign of God and the gospel of Christ will penetrate our devastated world only through love, which is paramount over every other power or force.

In the midst of the increasing violence, injustice, cruelty, and cold-heartedness of our time, love must be revealed: a love that towers above all earth's mountains, that shines more purely and brightly than all the stars in the sky, that is mightier than all earthquakes and volcanic eruptions, that is greater than all world powers and rulers, that works more powerfully in history than all catastrophes, wars, and revolutions, that is more alive than all life and natural forces in creation. Above everything in nature and within all history, love shows itself to be the ultimate power of the Almighty, the ultimate greatness of his heart, the ultimate revelation of his spirit.

1 John 4:8

The experience of God is love – love that overcomes everything that opposes it. Love is the energy of the new creation, the spirit of God's coming reign, the sole element in the new world he is building, and the herald of a new era. It is the organic strength of unity, the shaping of a new humanity. This love becomes reality in the church of Jesus Christ, through its unity. The church is built up through gathering people together; whoever does not gather with her scatters. Her life consists in uniting; whoever stands apart from this unity remains in death. Life comes through the spirit of Jesus Christ, who establishes the church's task in the midst of this fallen age. In the church we may experience God through Christ. In this fellowship of perfect love, God's spirit brings the perfect justice of Christ's kingdom to this earth. ⤳

1 Cor. 13:13

Eph. 2:14-22

Source: *Innenland: Ein Wegweiser in de Seele der Bible* (1936), 20–22, 213–215. Trans. Emmy Barth Maendel and Peter Mommsen.

Get a free ebook of Arnold's complete masterwork Innerland *at* plough.com/innerland.

ERIC K. TAYLOR

Ramadan

IT WAS THE MONTH OF RAMADAN, the month when Muslims fast. From the day's first light, when they could tell a white thread from a black one, until evening hid the difference again, they did not eat, did not drink, and – here in rural Liberia – did not even swallow their own spit.

We were three thousand miles from home when the telegram came. My mother's father had died. From Gbapa, three miles away, five dark-skinned Mandingo men came walking to our house. Students from her English class, a class in a building with mud-brick walls and a tin roof that pinged in the rain. She drove to them several nights each week, teaching them to write "hut" and "mat" and "cat," drawing little pictures beside the words. But this day, they came to her, walking over dusty, rust-colored roads, under the African sun. They came to sit with her, to offer what comfort they could.

We could not offer them water or coke or tea. For a few hours they sat, talking in soft voices, stepping out occasionally to spit. Then home again . . . waiting for black and white to merge back into one.

Someone once asked Jesus what it meant to love our neighbor. He said it was to be those men.

Eric K. Taylor, author of Using Folktales *(Cambridge University, 2000), is currently working on several novels for children.*

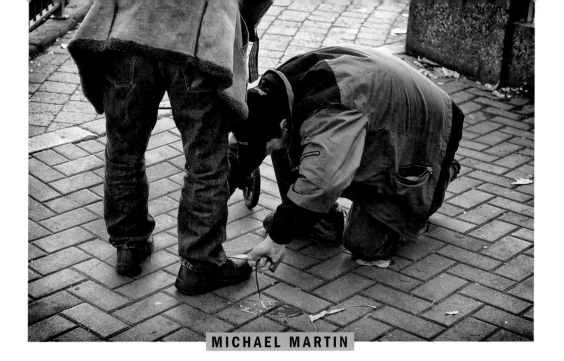

MICHAEL MARTIN

Activist Mystics

In Search of an Integrated Life

W hat are mystics good for? If you follow prevailing wisdom, the answer is clear: not much. To really get things done in the world, we're told, we need men and women of action.

Modern Christianity has bought into this idea. Much of medieval Christianity, too, affirmed the dichotomy between "contemplation" and "service"; it just valued the former over the latter. Religious orders that had a charism of "contemplation" were thought to be following the example of Mary over Martha, choosing "the better part" (Luke 10:38–42).

But there are clues that this polarized way of understanding the Christian life is wrong. Some of those clues lie in the text of the New Testament itself. The Lord withdrew to pray before his great works: before the calling of the disciples and the Sermon on the Mount, before walking on the sea, before his Passion. Other clues lie in the lives of those who took Christ as their template, who sought to follow him with their whole selves.

Where, after all, have many of those who have been most effective in the world gotten their ability to carry on? What is the source of the stubborn grace with which these people have persisted in doing good? To answer this question, I'd like to look at three very different examples: the spirituality of the Beguines, the life and work of the metaphysical poet Henry Vaughan, and the mystical activism of Simone Weil.

The Beguines

During the thirteenth century, partially because the fourth Lateran Council (1215) forbade the organization of any new religious

Michael Martin is an author and assistant professor of English and philosophy at Marygrove College.

orders, and partially because of the church's new emphasis on preaching and the "cure of souls," Christian Europe found itself with a better-catechized laity. Religious orders, however, expected a dowry to be paid for those entering the convent, so those without sufficient means to match their devotion were barred from the cloister.[1] In addition, a "woman surplus" made marriage impossible for many young women.[2]

Enter the Beguines. Especially active in the Low Countries and France, the Beguines were a lay movement of women (their male counterparts, far less numerous, were known as Beghards) who joined in communities in order to develop a life of deep prayer combined with a commitment to serving the sick, the dying, and the poor.

Though they adopted uniform habits of dress similar to women in consecrated religious life, the Beguines didn't make any formal vows and could come and go as they pleased – even maintaining their own households if they could afford to. The church exercised far less supervision over the spiritual lives of Beguines than over those in monastic life, and their confessors and spiritual directors were, often, in sympathy with the movement. Meister Eckhart, for example, was the spiritual director for a community of Beguines, and his mystical spirituality had much in common with theirs.

With a more tenuous relationship to authority came a greater degree of independence in their spiritual and practical lives. As a result, the Beguine way of life often confused contemporaries. "There are among us," wrote Gilbert of Tournai (ca. 1200–1284), "women whom we have no idea what to call, ordinary women or nuns, because they live neither in the world nor out of it."[3] Their otherness – not to mention their independence – led them into trouble with church authorities on occasion, and in 1310, it resulted in the fiercely courageous and uncompromising Beguine mystic Marguerite Porete being burned at the stake as a heretic.

Along with other thirteenth-century Beguines and former Beguines, such as Mechthild of Magdeburg, Hadewijch of Antwerp,[4] and Beatrice of Nazareth, Porete wrote in a variety of literary genres. These women developed a theological aesthetics grounded in love. Their mystical writings, like the Song of Songs, depict a spirituality of the bridal chamber. Theirs is a spirituality of complete abandonment: love serves as both their way of knowing and their way of acting. This love appears in the world as care for the poor. They understand God by forsaking understanding. They transcend the idea of ascent to God by degrees, instead uniting themselves to him directly through love. They take Augustine's "Love God and do what you will" seriously – which is what alarmed the ecclesiastical authorities of their times. As Hans Urs von Balthasar observes, "Lovers are the ones who know most about God; the theologian must listen to them."[5] Unfortunately, the theologians of the medieval period did not tend to be big listeners, especially with regard to women.

While we possess a great store of the mystical literature of the Beguines, documentation of the service-oriented aspects of their lives

1. Emilie Zum Brunn and Georgette Epiney-Burgard, introduction to *Women Mystics in the Middle Ages*, (Paragon, 1989), xx–xxi.
2. Walter Simons, *Cities of Ladies: Beguine Communities in the Medieval Low Countries, 1200–1565* (University of Pennsylvania, 2001), 109.
3. Quoted in Carol Neel, "The Origins of the Beguines," *Signs* 14, no. 2, (Winter 1989): 321–341, at 323.
4. There may have been either one or two women known by this name.
5. Hans Urs von Balthasar, *Love Alone Is Credible* [1963], (Ignatius, 2004), 12.

is sparse. We know they set up hospitals and schools, took special care of lepers, did what we would now call hospice work, and served the poor. We know that their ministry was almost totally devoted to the care of women. We know that Beguines worked in farming and animal husbandry, and as weavers, tailors, embroiderers, and launderers, among other trades. Unlike their counterparts in the cloister, Beguines were free, as James of Vitry noted in 1216, to "live by the work of their own hand."[6] But they didn't really like to write about it. Instead, they emphasized their encounters with God, for without these encounters, their lives would mean nothing.

The good works of the Beguines, they would say, were not their own but God's. To draw attention to these works would be prideful. Their participation in these works was merely a product of their complete abandonment to God and his love. As Mechthild of Magdeburg

6. Quoted by Simons, *Cities of Ladies*, 68.

prays, "Ah, dear Lord, have mercy on one who has been consumed here in the fire of your love and has been absorbed in your humility and has been annihilated in all things."[7] The Beguines were absorbed in humility. The only cause they had to promote was abandonment to God.

Henry Vaughan

When the first English Civil War ended in summer of 1646, a Royalist lieutenant, Henry Vaughan, aged twenty-five, returned home to Brecon, Wales, to convalesce, having suffered imprisonment for his defense of King Charles I. Within a year, his dear younger brother William died. On January 30, 1649, the Parliamentarian government of Oliver Cromwell beheaded the king for whom he had fought. The young Welshman was ripe for a spiritual crisis.

And he got one.

7. Mechthild of Magdeburg, *The Flowing Light of the Godhead* (Paulist, 1998), 252.

Marguerite Porete
The noble Virtue of Charity and how she obeys none other than Love

Charity obeys no created thing except Love.

Charity possesses nothing of her own, and should she possess something she does not say that it belongs to her.

Charity abandons her own need and attends to that of others.

Charity asks no payment from any creature for some good or pleasure that she has accomplished.

Charity has no shame, nor fear, nor anxiety. She is so upright she cannot bow on account of anything that might happen to her.

Charity neither makes nor takes account of anything under the sun, for the whole world is only refuse and leftovers.

Charity gives to all what she possesses of worth, without retaining anything for herself, and with this she often promises what she does not possess through her great largesse, in the hope that the more she gives the more remains in her.

Charity is such a wise merchant that she earns profits everywhere where others lose, and she escapes the bonds that bind others and thus she has great multiplicity of what pleases Love.

And note that the one who would have perfect charity must be mortified in the affections of the life of the spirit through the work of charity.

From Marguerite Porete, *The Mirror of Simple Souls,* trans. Ellen L. Babinsky (Paulist, 1993), 82.

But his reading of John Donne and, especially, George Herbert during his convalescence gave him a vocabulary for exploring his own encounter with God. In the two installations of his *Silex Scintillans* ("the sparking flint," 1650 and 1655), he gives voice to this encounter. He also adds something unusual (in his time) to the language of poetry: the natural world. Critics have been fond of categorizing Vaughan as a harbinger of the nature mysticism often attributed to the Romantic poets, but this is a rather ham-handed association. Nature does not interest Vaughan in itself, as a thing to be observed and enjoyed. Rather, it is important because it reveals and participates in God. And, as he writes in the poem "Rules and Lessons," the creation indeed speaks of the Creator:

> To heighten thy *Devotions,* and keep low
> All mutinous thoughts, what business e'r thou hast
> Observe God in his works; here *fountains* flow,
> *Birds* sing, *Beasts* feed, *Fish* leap, and th' *Earth*
> stands fast;
>> Above are restless *motions,* running *Lights,*
>> Vast Circling *Azure,* giddy *Clouds,* days, nights.

Henry Vaughan was the identical twin of Thomas Vaughan, the Anglican priest, and both were interested in the scientific and religious ideas then seeping into Britain from the Continent, particularly the idea that there is a synergy between the spiritual world, the human body, and the creation. Both Vaughans believed in the doctrine of signatures in medicine (the idea that herbs resemble the part of the body that they are able to cure) as they believed in biblical typology: the idea that God's wisdom could reveal itself to the attentive reader of nature and scripture. These interests manifest in the writings of both brothers, but they also made their way into their working lives – they were physicians. In his poetry, Henry adopts the same ethos he held as a doctor: poetry as physic for the soul,

leading readers into a relationship with God.

Vaughan's interest in medicine was of a piece with his attention to the natural world, his love for God, and his care for others. He lived, that is, an integrated life. He did not have one brain for science and another for faith. Rather, science and faith, in his eyes, revealed the same essence.

However, very little about Vaughan's life as a doctor is known to us. As with the Beguines, the inner life with God he describes in his poetry was the only thing he considered worth committing to posterity.

Simone Weil

Simone Weil (1909–1943) is one of the most fascinating – and intimidating – religious figures of the twentieth century. Previously an atheist, philosopher, pacifist, activist, social critic, and teacher, Weil, in her search for truth, became a factory worker, farm laborer, soldier, and mystic – and her search very nearly made her a Catholic. During World War II, Weil worked for the French Resistance in England, refusing to permit herself more food than was available to those in occupied France. She contracted tuberculosis, but despite doctors' instructions, she did not eat more. Finally, she died, causing the coroner to record that "the deceased did kill and slay herself by refusing to eat whilst the balance of her mind was disturbed." In truth, she was anything but disturbed, as Albert Camus testified in calling her "the only great spirit of our times." The times were disturbed. To be the only sane person in a mad world is to be considered mad.

Unlike the Beguines and Henry Vaughan, Weil was an activist before her mystical encounters with God. Yet, though she was ethnically Jewish, with parents who were atheists, Christianity had always seemed to be a part of her. "While the very name of God had no part in my thoughts," she wrote, "with regard to the problems of this world and this life, I shared the Christian conception in an explicit and rigorous manner, with the most specific notions it involves."[8] This sensibility led her to seek solidarity with the poor, the marginalized, and the afflicted. And desire led to deeds. Initially, her social activism guided her to communism, but, though she was known in that milieu as "the Red Virgin," she became disenchanted with radical politics. "It is not religion but revolution which is the opium of the people," she concluded.[9] Only Christ possessed the truth she had intuited all her life.

Weil's gradual journey to the cross was the product of an important tool of the mystics, and one that she employed from an early

8. Simone Weil, *Waiting for God* (Harper, 2009), 22.

9. Simone Weil, *An Anthology*, ed. Sián Miles (Grove, 1986), 160.

Simone Weil
An Encounter

He entered my room and said: "You poor wretch, who understand nothing and know nothing – come with me and I will teach you of things you have no idea of." I followed him.

He led me into a church. It was new and ugly. He led me before the altar and said: "Kneel." I told him: "I have not been baptized." He said: "Fall down on your knees before this place, with love, as before the place where truth exists." I obeyed.

He led me out, and up to a garret from whose open window one could see the whole town, some wooden scaffoldings, and the river where boats were unloading. He made me sit down.

We were alone. He talked. Now and then somebody else would come in, join in the conversation, then go away again.

It was no longer winter; it was not yet spring. The trees' branches were bare and without buds, in a cold air full of sunshine.

The light rose, shone bright, and then faded, and the stars and the moon shone through the window. Then the dawn rose once again.

Sometimes he paused and took some bread from a cupboard, and we shared it. That bread truly had the taste of bread. I have never found that taste again.

He poured wine for me and for himself, which tasted of the sun and of the soil on which that city was built.

Sometimes we lay down on the wooden floor, and the sweetness of sleep descended on me. Then I woke up, and drank the light of the sun.

He had promised me teaching, but he taught me nothing. We talked in a rambling way about all sorts of things, as old friends do.

One day he said to me, "Now go away." I threw myself down, clung to his knees, begged him not to send me away. But he flung me out toward the stairs. I descended them as if unconscious, as if my heart was torn in shreds. I walked through the streets, and then I realized that I had no idea where that house was.

I have never tried to find it again. I saw that he had come for me by mistake. My place is not in that garret. It is anywhere, in a prison cell, in some bourgeois parlour full of trinkets and red plush, in a station waiting room. No matter where, but not in that garret.

Sometimes I cannot keep myself from repeating, in fear and compunction, a little of what he said to me. How am I to know if I remember it correctly? He is not there to tell me.

I well know that he doesn't love me. How could he love me? And yet there is something deep in me, some point of myself, which cannot prevent itself from thinking, with fear and trembling, that perhaps, in spite of everything, he does love me.

From Simone Weil, *First and Last Notebooks*, trans. Richard Rees (Oxford University, 1970), 65–66.

age: the ability to pay scrupulous attention to whatever or whoever was before her. "Attention," she writes, "is the rarest and purest form of generosity."[10] And it was this attention that God began more and more to capture. In 1937, Weil visited Assisi. In the Basilica of Santa Maria degli Angeli, where Saint Francis had prayed, "something stronger than I was compelled me for the first time in my life to go down on my knees."[11] For the first time, she prayed. During Holy Week the following year, she attended liturgical services. "In the course of these services," she wrote, "the thought of the Passion of Christ entered into my being once and for all." Later – like Vaughan – Weil discovered George Herbert's poetry. Her attention to the poem "Love (III)" resulted in an experience in which, she said, "Christ himself came down and took possession of me."

For the rest of her short life, her activism and her writing were increasingly shot through with mystical and religious threads, permeated by her encounter with Christ.

Weil was painfully aware of the spiritual and psychological traps inherent to the ego's involvement in activism, writing, "God is not present, even if we invoke him, where the afflicted are merely regarded as an occasion for doing good." For Weil, it wasn't enough to feel sympathy for factory workers, soldiers, or farm laborers. She needed to suffer alongside them, to help bear their burdens. Is this not what Christ did through the Incarnation? Nietzsche wrote, with some justification, that "in truth, there was only one Christian, and he died on the cross." Nietzsche is lucky he never met Simone Weil. She would have rattled him. She should rattle everyone.

Paul the Apostle, perhaps the prototype for both the mystic and the missionary, clearly saw no division between the two vocations. The man who "was snatched up to Paradise to hear words which no man may speak" (2 Cor. 12:4) was also shipwrecked, beaten, scourged, and eventually beheaded for spreading the gospel and founding churches throughout the Mediterranean. Others throughout history also lived rich inner lives of mystical union with God complemented by lives of service or mission, what we now might call activism. Among them are Francis of Assisi, Teresa of Ávila, the seventeenth-century leader of the Philadelphian Society Jane Lead (who modeled her mission on that of Paul), and Dorothy Day of the Catholic Worker movement. As the Russian philosopher and mystic Vladimir Soloviev observed, Christ "did not send his apostles into the solitude of the desert, but into the world to conquer it and subject it to the kingdom which is not of this world."[12]

Not everyone is called to the celibacy and service of the Beguines, not everyone is called to the poetic and medical vocation of Henry Vaughan, and not everyone is called to the uncompromising witness of Simone Weil. But everyone is called. What the Beguines, Vaughan, and Weil provide for us are models of the integrated life, a life whose inner reality is mirrored in the individual's outer work in the world. Grounded in an experience of God's own love, mystical activism is the quiet revolution that without force, compulsion, or shaming transforms the world into the kingdom. ⤙

10. Simone Weil to Joë Bousquet, April 13, 1942. *Correspondance* (Éditions l'Âge d'Homme, 1982), 18.

11. Weil, *Waiting for God,* 26. Subsequent quotes from Weil: ibid., 34, 27, 93.

12. Vladimir Soloviev, *Russia and the Universal Church* (Geoffrey Bles, 1948), 39.

WAITING IN SILENCE
Wisdom from an Early Quaker

ISAAC PENINGTON

After the mind is in some measure turned to the Lord – his quickenings felt, his seed beginning to arise and spring up in the heart – then the flesh is to be silent before him, and the soul to wait upon him (and for his further appearings) in that measure of life which is already revealed.

Now, this is a great thing: to know flesh silenced, to feel the reasoning thoughts and discourses of the fleshly mind stilled, and the wisdom, light, and guidance of God's spirit waited for. For we are to come into the poverty of self, into the abasedness, into the nothingness, into the silence of our spirit before the Lord; into the putting off of all our knowledge, wisdom, understanding, abilities, all that we are, have done, or can do, out of this measure of life, into which we are to travel, that we may be clothed and filled with the nature, Spirit, and power of the Lord.

God is to be worshipped in spirit, in his own power and life, and this is at his own disposal. His church is a gathering in the Spirit. If any speak there, they must speak as the oracle of God, as the vessel out of which God speaks; as the trumpet out of which he gives the sound. Therefore there is to be a waiting in silence till the Spirit of the Lord move to speak, and also give words to speak. For we are not to speak our own words, or in our own wisdom or time; but the Spirit's words, in the Spirit's wisdom and time, which is when he moves and gives to speak.

Eye hath not seen, nor ear heard, neither hath entered into the heart how and what things God reveals to his children by his Spirit, when they wait upon him in his pure fear, and worship and converse with him in spirit; for then the fountain of the great deep is unsealed, and the everlasting springs surely give up the pure and living water. ➤

Source: "A brief account concerning silent meetings; the nature, use, intent, and benefit of them," published 1680 (text lightly modernized).

Isaac Penington (1616–1679), the oldest son of a Lord Mayor of London, became a leader in the Quaker movement founded by his younger contemporary George Fox; shunned by family and friends for his convictions, he was imprisoned six times.

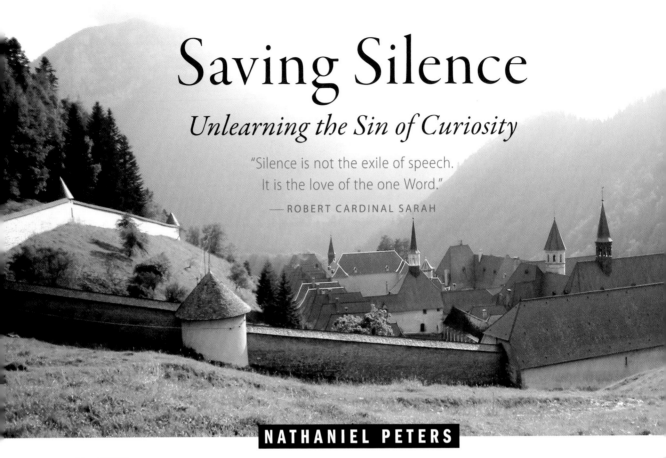

Saving Silence

Unlearning the Sin of Curiosity

"Silence is not the exile of speech.
It is the love of the one Word."

— ROBERT CARDINAL SARAH

NATHANIEL PETERS

A world of silence: Grande Chartreuse Monastery, Grenoble, France

I GO TO LOOK UP a newspaper article on a dispute between a high-ranking judge and a popular journalist. In the middle of the article, I find some unexpected headlines inviting me to click. The frankness of this would-be enticement makes it laughable, and gives me little pause as I continue on with my article. But it serves as a reminder of the noise that characterizes our present age. Sin is not only easy to find, but it comes after you. We are prompted and guided to distraction, coaxed into desiring things we never thought we needed or needed to know.

Earlier Christians had a word for this: curiosity. Curiosity might be the besetting sin of our time. On the face of it, such a statement seems absurd, or perhaps it belongs to a more legalistic period of Christian life that modern believers have happily outgrown. Curiosity is the desire to understand, which we consider a good thing; schools and responsible parents encourage it, and our economy rewards it. But earlier Christians recognized that the desire for knowledge is not necessarily pure. This should not surprise us, since we recognize that our other appetites can go astray in a number of ways. In his *Intellectual Appetite: A Theological Grammar,* Paul Griffiths notes that all Latin Christians from Tertullian through Bossuet in the seventeenth century recognized curiosity as a disordered appetite for knowledge that we do not have or need to know. This they distinguished from studiousness, an eager and rightly ordered pursuit of the truth.

In *On the Trinity,* Saint Augustine of Hippo makes the distinction this way: The studious

Nathaniel Peters recently completed a PhD in theology from Boston College.

are prompted by a love of what they know. The curious hate what they do not know with "anxious hatred," wanting to reduce the number of unknowns to zero, to extinguish them. Curiosity wants new knowledge or intimacy with something so it can use that knowledge to control and dominate. It is the appetite for the ownership of new knowledge. It is concerned with novelty and knowing what others do not know.

The studious want to participate lovingly in what they know and respond to it as a gift, with intimacy. Saint Thomas Aquinas calls studiousness a kind of temperance, a moderation of our natural desires, like chastity or moderation in our food and drink. By contrast, the philosopher Hans Blumenberg notes, the curious seek their enjoyment not in the objects of their knowledge or study, but ultimately only in themselves.

This may seem like splitting hairs, but we see it all the time when on the internet or even as we wait to pay for our groceries in the supermarket. The headlines we see appeal to our propensity to gossip, lust, and anger. They call us to look at beautiful bodies, read the juicy news of the downfall of others, and fuel our rage at the triumph of our political enemies. But the handmaiden to all these sins is that small desire to know more when we have no good reason for knowing it. Our study of our faith and the information proper to our vocations have a gathering effect. They concentrate the mind and, with effort, create clarity.

Curiosity, by contrast, scatters and produces noise, not fruit.

The noise of curiosity is one strain of the broader cacophony in our culture. Even people with little concern for the virtue of studiousness or the health of the soul have begun to take notice. There are now TED talks and popular articles on the ways in which internet pornography physically changes the brain. Just using a smartphone shapes your intellectual habits, albeit with less grave consequences. *The Atlantic* reported recently on the way in which silence has become a luxury good, especially for those who upgrade to the luxury lounges in airports and purchase expensive noise-canceling headphones. The latter are perhaps the best symbol of our environment: canceling out the world around us the better to fill ourselves with the pure sound of our own choice.

Christian authors such as James K. A. Smith and Rod Dreher have called attention to our need for weaning from our devices, a practice Dreher calls "technological asceticism." Now Robert Cardinal Sarah, the former Catholic archbishop of the Guinean capital Conakry and current prefect for the Vatican's Congregation for Divine Worship and the Discipline of the Sacraments, offers a strong antidote with *The Power of Silence: Against the Dictatorship of Noise,* an extended interview with the French journalist Nicolas Diat. The book is not a theological argument, but distilled, searing wisdom drawn from patristic writers such as Isaac the Syrian and Gregory the Great as well as modern authors such as Thomas Merton and Maurice Zundel. It should be read slowly and deliberately.

For Sarah, silence is an open space in which encounter with God is possible, and is therefore the nexus of many aspects of the spiritual life. We tend to think of silence as the absence of noise, in which case silence is a primarily negative attribute. However, Sarah writes, "Silence is not an absence. On the contrary, it is the manifestation of a presence, the most intense of all presences." The silence of God is the simple and quiet expression of his being, the eternal movement of the persons of the Trinity in their relations. Hence Sarah writes: "The silence of God is a form of speech. His Word is solitude. The solitude of God is not an absence, it is his very being, his silent transcendence." Or in the words of Saint John of the Cross: "The Father spoke one Word, which was his Son, and this Word he always speaks in eternal silence, and in silence it must be heard by the soul."

Creation itself, Sarah writes, is a kind of silent word God speaks, and by creating men and women in his image and likeness, he invites them into a silent encounter. Thus from the human standpoint, silence is, as Diat puts it, "above all the attitude of someone who listens." The French word *disponibilité* captures this well. It means availability, receptivity, the "Here I am" of Samuel called before the Lord in the temple in the darkness of the night. It is reminiscent as well of Solomon's request for a heart that listens to God, for the silence that is the beginning of wisdom.

This silence at the heart of our being is an important aspect of the likeness of God in us, the place where we become more like him. Sarah writes:

> When he drapes himself in silence, as God himself dwells in a great silence, man is close to heaven, or, rather, he allows God to manifest himself in him. . . . At the heart of man there is an innate silence, for God abides in the innermost part of every person. God is silence, and this divine silence dwells in man.

The task of the spiritual life, then, is to cultivate that silent receptivity to God and to those we meet. Though Sarah does not map out a program for doing this, he points toward three things. First, he says, it is absurd to talk about interior silence without exterior silence. We need to follow Christ's example and spend time alone with God, minimizing exterior distractions. Second, Sarah recommends the kind of close study of scripture that Christians have undertaken for centuries, commonly called *lectio divina*. This is not an academic study of the text, but rather a way of meditating on the text that uses verses and themes as spurs toward prayer.

Third, Sarah says that we must be ready to encounter and quiet "the interior turmoil" we find within ourselves: "the agitations, the busyness, the easy pleasures," the noise of our own ego and memories of our past sins. In the final chapter of the book, Cardinal Sarah speaks with Dom Dysmus de Lassus, the Minister General of the Carthusian Order, the Catholic Church's most strictly contemplative monks. Lassus notes that the disquiet we feel in silence comes not from the silence, but from what it reveals. We have to learn how to tame "the menagerie that lives inside us if we want the wild animals to be able to leave us in silence someday." This, he says, is not so much a matter of struggling against our unwanted thoughts, "but rather of unceasingly returning to God."

The refusal to do this lies at the heart of the culture of noise Cardinal Sarah decries. Our culture's aversion to silence is an aversion to the real questions of life and the things with which we must wrestle as part of the human condition, chief among these the question of God. Here is where curiosity leads us into dissipated internal noise instead of deepening the knowledge that leads us to God. The cardinal writes:

> For someone who is far from God, silence is a difficult confrontation with his own self

INSIGHT ON SILENCE

"The greatest things are accomplished in silence – not in the clamor and display of superficial eventfulness, but in the deep clarity of inner vision; in the almost imperceptible start of decision, in quiet overcoming and hidden sacrifice. Spiritual conception happens when the heart is quickened by love, and the free will stirs to action. The silent forces are the strong forces."

Romano Guardini, *The Lord*

and with the rather dismal realities that are at the bottom of our soul. Hence, man enters a mentality that resembles a denial of reality. He gets drunk on all sorts of noises so as to forget who he is. Postmodern man seeks to anesthetize his own atheism.

Noise thus becomes "a whirlwind that avoids facing itself" and a kind of tranquilizer that keeps many from confronting wonder, God, and the demands of their own emptiness.

In response, Sarah urges Christians to cultivate silence in their corporate piety and worship. He echoes Thomas Merton's call to form communities where homes and classrooms – despite their activity – become sanctuaries of silence. We need not think we have to share the intimate details of our spiritual lives with groups or pump ourselves with feelings to worship God.

SOME OF THE MOST SILENT Christians to worship God are the Carthusian monks. They live as a community of hermits, praying together daily but spending most of their remaining time in solitude. Their motto: "The cross stands while the world turns." In over nine hundred years they have never undergone a major reform of their congregation, because it has never been necessary. Their motherhouse lies in a valley in the Chartreuse Mountains next to the French Alps, which gave the order its name. The heart of Carthusian life is the Night Office, their midnight service of psalms and readings that lasts more than two hours and is conducted in darkness. Its soul, Dom de Lassus writes, is the thirst for God. Carthusian silence is pregnant with desire:

> The contemplative soul that has learned the language of the divine Bridegroom, although it never hears it as one hears human speech, still learns gradually to notice its traces everywhere. This soul then resembles a loving woman who knows that she is deeply loved, waiting to meet in the evening the man whom she loves.

I experienced something of this some years ago when I visited the Grande Chartreuse. The bus dropped me off at the foot of a steep road. As I climbed, the air was sweet and thick enough to cut. I came to a small complex that used to serve as an infirmary, office, and residence for some of the monks. Now it is a museum in which visitors can experience a taste of Carthusian life, since they are not admitted into the main building. Every cell is made with rich wood and looks out at the soaring mountains. When I climbed further up, past cows pastured before the crags, I saw the Grande Chartreuse itself. I put my eye to a keyhole and spied a Carthusian practicing chant in a chapel. The only opening for visitors was in the outer wall. I entered and discovered a chapel with the Blessed Sacrament and a sign inviting me to encounter God, who waited for me here in the great silence.

Bruce Herman, *Behind School Street*, 1984

A Lens

That All, which always is all everywhere
                                        —Donne

Not that we think he is confined to us,
Locked in the box of our religious rites,
Or curtained by these frail cathedral walls,
No church is broad or creed compendious
Enough. All thought's a narrowing of sites.
Before him every definition fails,
Words fall and flutter into emptiness,
Like motes of dust within his spaciousness.

Not that we summon him, but that he lends
The very means whereby he might be known,
Till this opacity of stone on stone,
This trace of light and music on the air,
This sacred space itself becomes a lens
To sense his presence who is everywhere.

MALCOLM GUITE

SR. DOMINIC MARY HEATH

Giving God Our Attention

Learning the Virtue of Studiousness

Curiosity is a sin (page 32). But what about our inborn desire to understand things – is that all bad? No, said Thomas Aquinas: it comes from God and can lead us to him. Aquinas had a name for it: *studiousness*. This virtue isn't just for scholars – it matters just as much to mechanics, outdoorsmen, and artisans. And in the end, it belongs most of all to the childlike.

ON A CLOISTER WALL in Florence there's an old, fifteenth-century fresco of Dominic de Guzmán. The Spanish saint, founder of the Dominican Order, sits in a posture of easy grace, seemingly unaware of his surroundings. His attentive gaze draws our eyes to the object he holds – an open book. Dominic is at study.

The portrait is idyllic, charming even. It's also misleading. The real drama of the painting takes place in the plane beyond Dominic's figure. There we see Christ crowned with thorns,

Sr. Dominic Mary Heath is a novice with the cloistered Dominican nuns at the Monastery of Our Lady of Grace in North Guilford, CT.

blindfolded, and mocked. Spittle streams toward his face, while the hands of unseen assailants hang in midair – impossibly – heightening the inhumanity of the scene. In the foreground opposite Dominic sits the sorrowful Virgin, her own eyes cast down and heavy with grief.

The effect of Fra Angelico's *Mocking of Christ* is stunning, but also confusing. For a contemporary audience it raises a real problem: What does study have to do with holy sorrow?

Most of us will have a hard time answering this question because the world in which we live has forgotten something Dominic and the medievals knew, something about the very human act of study. What we've lost, in fact, is the virtue of studiousness. And there are very good reasons for Christians in particular to be concerned with its recovery.

As the religion of the Word made flesh, Christianity consecrates the human intellectual life in a unique way. But not all Christians are aware of this, others aren't quite convinced, and very few have any idea where to begin. But the virtue of studiousness shouldn't be strange and intimidating to us. It should be as familiar as our own creatureliness.

Our Need-to-Know Basis

Each one of us has a natural desire for knowledge that has nothing to do with whether we consider ourselves the intellectual type or pride ourselves on being readers. Our desire for knowledge is fundamentally human and so deeply seated that Saint Thomas Aquinas – a spiritual son of Dominic – compares it to the body's desire for its own natural goods: just as the body craves food and sex, the soul craves knowledge. In fact, because the soul is the highest, and governing, part of us, its desires are arguably greater and more urgent than those of the body. Put simply, we really, really want to know things.

This is where study comes in. Study is the keen application of the mind to truth. It is the way we feed our hunger for knowledge. And because this desire is God-given, study itself shares in the urgency of our lifelong search for happiness. Unless we apply our minds to truth, we will never be happy.

The idea that study leads to happiness may seem far-fetched to anyone who has never been happy while studying. The fact is that most of us think of study as something we really ought to do, something we wish we enjoyed, or something that would make us better versions of ourselves. In other words, we think study is for the mind what routine exercise is for the body – an amoral exertion with no lasting value. If this were true, study would make us happy like being in good shape makes us "happy." And, currently, some of us might feel either a little guilty, or a little self-satisfied, about our level of performance.

It may surprise us, then, to learn that, in the Christian vision of things, study is neither a personal lifestyle choice nor a habit of self-care – it's a moral virtue.

The Virtue Called Studiousness

This brings us to studiousness, which is, technically, the word we want when talking about study as a moral virtue. For most of us, "studiousness" probably has associations with dusty books, library stacks, and pale-faced scholars who seldom see the light of day. Basically, studiousness sounds a lot like diligence, concentration, and hard work. And, in a sense, studiousness is these things – but only in a secondary sense. This is a fascinating insight we get from Aquinas.

According to Aquinas, the virtue of studiousness is, indirectly, a spur to the body whose natural weakness and desire for comfort would otherwise keep the mind from pursuing

studiousness makes us happy by making us, actually, good.

Because studiousness directs our minds to good things in the right measure, it allows us to develop a taste for what is truly interesting in the world around us – say, Homer's *Iliad* or the principles of algebraic topology – and a dislike for what is merely titillating, sensational, or distracting. Without studiousness, our otherwise wholesome desire for knowledge would fall into the crude distortions that characterize the vice of curiosity. Some things are worth knowing, other things may not be worth knowing, and still others are definitely not worth knowing.

That's the reason we can't talk about study without also talking about our creatureliness. Creatureliness presumes an order inherent in the very nature of things and a goal that attracts all our desires. By directing our natural desire for knowledge toward this goal, studiousness brings a particular beauty to the soul, the beauty of spiritual clarity. It endows the soul with the same "moderate and fitting proportion" that characterizes all fundamentally honest things.[1] It makes us more fully human, more ourselves.

Put this way, studiousness is really very attractive. And already we can anticipate an opening for the spiritual dimension of the human person. What, after all, do we mean by

Fra Angelico, *Mocking of Christ,* fresco, Convent of San Marco, Florence, Italy. Saint Dominic de Guzmán (*bottom right*) reads the story of Jesus' Passion (*shown center*), while Mary grieves.

its own proper work. But studiousness is not primarily about getting the body to try harder. Instead, it is properly concerned with getting the will to desire correctly. And since it has to do with our desire for knowledge in particular, studiousness is the moral virtue that attracts us to what is worth knowing (the true and good) and, conversely, repels us from what is not (the false and perverted).

This is why Aquinas can say that studiousness is actually a kind of temperance – temperance for the mind. Just as the virtue of temperance is a habit of moderating our natural appetite for bodily pleasure, studiousness is a habit of moderating our natural desire for knowledge. Self-imposed moderation of this sort doesn't mean censorship or close-mindedness. It means that studiousness – like every moral virtue – inclines us to what is reasonable, while reason itself directs us to what is good. In other words, "an order inherent in the very nature of things"? Toward what goal is studiousness directing us? As it turns out, there are competing, and even contradictory, answers to these questions.

Can Studiousness Lead Us to God?

Secular modernity has its own beliefs about the order inherent in the very nature of things, and the first of these assumptions is that there are no spiritual natures in things. Its view of the human person is essentially materialistic and, consequently, individualistic. That's why its moral code can so seamlessly unite relativism to utilitarianism: Do what you want! But be useful! Even if we resist the idea that humans are only matter, the fact is that all of us have been shaped by these deep-set cultural imperatives.

A materialist, therapeutic culture like this can give only two reasons for study. Study is either a way for each of us to express our own distinctive personality or a way for us to produce something useful for the world.

> Contemplation is not a waste of time – it's a supremely good use of time.

Ideally, it's both. This explains, for example, why higher education today has become an increasingly bizarre mash-up of obscure fields of study on the one hand and highly technical, professional degrees on the other. Cafeteria-style education – seemingly all-pervasive – makes perfect sense if the order inherent in the very nature of things is actually a dictatorship of our material and psychological urges.

Studiousness in this context is a "virtue" only in the sense that it is a habit we need to achieve our cultural goals of originality and self-sufficiency. Studiousness, understood as a virtue directing us toward a moral goal we call "the Good," is essentially lost.

Not surprisingly, Christianity has a very different understanding of the order inherent in things than does secular modernity. That order, set in the sinews of creation, accords with the pattern of the eternal Logos: the intelligibility of reality reveals to us the eternal Word of God (Prov. 8:22–31). That's why Christianity also offers us a very different model of human flourishing: Human persons are not the sum of our merely biological and psychological parts. Our wants are not only material and emotional. Instead, our deepest desires flow from the highest part of us, the rational soul which has been created *ad imago Dei* and is capable of union with God by grace. This means that, even though we have many legitimate desires for transitory goods in life, what each of us really, truly wants is to pay attention to God. And paying attention to God is perhaps the best definition we can give, not only of the goal of studiousness, but also of that prayer called contemplation.

Essentially, contemplation is the goal of study just as rest is the goal of activity. Used in this sense, rest doesn't mean a kind of exhaustion or listless emptiness. The mind in the act of contemplation is said to rest because it finally possesses, and therefore enjoys, what it has eagerly sought. When the lover sees the beloved, frenetic and discursive activity ceases and amazement begins.

What Christianity understands, and pragmatic modernity cannot grasp, is that contemplation is not a waste of time – it's a supremely good use of time. In contemplation we participate in what the Christian philosopher Josef Pieper calls, "the loving, yearning, affirming bent toward that happiness which is the same as God himself, and which is the aim and purpose of all that happens in the world."[2] In other words, even our finite, temporal contemplation drifts steadily toward the eternal. That's why, according to Pieper, there are no "nonreligious" forms of contemplation in this world. All contemplation is holy contemplation. This side of heaven, contemplation is a heady mix of loving wonder and "unease in the face of the unattainable."[3]

But if Christianity is right on this point – if our creaturely desire for knowledge is, fundamentally, a desire to contemplate God – study itself is elevated to a new plane. It's no longer a boutique commodity for the privileged and self-indulgent or a practical tool for the ambitious and self-reliant. It's not even a method of self-mastery for the perfectionist. Instead, study is a diligent search made in anticipation of finding God. And this search takes us through the entire created order, through the hierarchy of things "visible and invisible," until we learn to pay attention to God in our own hearts.

Studiousness understood in this sense, as the virtue that holds the soul's attention to God and to all true things for God's sake, is clearly much more than bookishness. A mind directed to God is a mind disposed for contemplative wonder; it has a particular "veneration for concrete reality"[4] because it seeks the divine meaning behind everything it sees. Study has value precisely because it leads beyond itself, through contemplation, to God. This is how it makes us happy.

Mind and Body

The problem for most of us is that when we're told "happiness is contemplation," what we actually hear is "happiness is disembodied." And we simply can't get excited about the prospect of studying for the sake of contemplation because we know, intuitively, that real human happiness never excludes the body. That's why we should already be asking how realistic the virtue of studiousness is for real, embodied people: Doesn't study require a lot of time, silence, and

solitude? Is it really so human after all?

This critique would be fair if "studying" began only when we decided to sit down and thoughtfully think thoughts. This is how we usually imagine it. In actual fact, however, study starts with our five senses. Aquinas says that we "derive knowledge through sensibles,"[5] meaning that the body itself initiates the process of study through sight, touch, taste, hearing, and smell. This is just common sense, but it's also wonderful news: it means that the virtue of studiousness can be found in as many places, and in as many modes, as knowledge itself is found. And it means that (despite Descartes) studiousness can never be detached from the body.

Another way of saying this is that studiousness begins whenever we begin to observe *what is.* Whenever we pay attention to what is in front of us, we allow ourselves to be attracted to the good that is present in that thing. And we already know how studiousness moderates our natural desire for knowledge – by attracting us to the good according to reason. An essential part of studiousness, therefore, is precisely this embodied capacity to receive the world around us.

We don't have to read textbooks to experience this kind of studious absorption in reality. We can approach nature studiously whenever we see (smell, taste, touch, or hear) biological life unfolding. We can approach human community studiously whenever we observe meaningful patterns in history, politics, literature, or culture. We can approach the mechanical sciences studiously whenever we pay attention to the amazing way things work.

And we can approach the Christian faith itself studiously whenever we immerse ourselves in the sacred words of scripture and the sacred actions of liturgy.

If, in a real sense, studiousness makes demands on our bodies (time, attention, tranquility), this is only because it is carving out space in our lives for the truly human acts of reverence, delight, and praise. That's why it's a mistake to think that study belongs to the professionals. In actual fact, it belongs to the childlike. Blessed are the pure of heart, for they shall see God all around them.

Study and Service

It's purity of heart that enables us to see God in a world where contemplation is wounded by sin: we cannot study creation without being moved by God's own compassion for it. That's why we shouldn't be surprised when studiousness places real demands on us – demands of service.

> Study doesn't belong to the professionals. It belongs to the childlike.

Studiousness drives service, not in order to make creation more pleasing or useful to a consumer culture, but in order to conform creation to God's own, true idea of it. The discrepancy between the way God knows the world to be from eternity and the way the world is now through sin is why the truly studious will inevitably experience holy sorrow: there is a kinship here between the joy of contemplation and the tenderness of compassion that materialism will never fathom. Studying the wonderful design of the human body, for example, reminds us how disfiguring sickness is. And studying the qualities of a just society brings to light disintegration in our own communities. But this holy grief is not pessimism: it's the wound in us from which all the works of mercy flow out into the world.

Mercy, after all, begins when we take the needs of another as our own needs and their misery as our misery. It moves us to do for the "least of these" what we would do for ourselves. But to offer more than artificial consolation, mercy must know the truth about the world, the human person, and the Creator. Mercy needs studiousness. And studiousness, rather than providing an escape from the world in God, teaches us how to return into God for the sake of the world.

This orientation to merciful service is why study just looks different inside Christianity – why, in fact, it looks a lot like Dominic's contemplation of the suffering Christ. Christianity, after all, doesn't hawk a nondescript deity or a generic sense of god-dependency. It reveals a God who is at once intensely Trinitarian and, in the Person of the Eternal Word, really incarnate. In Christ, God takes a human face. And to contemplate this face is to be conformed to Mercy himself.

What is ultimately so extraordinary about Fra Angelico's *Mocking of Christ* is that the painting counters the human cruelty that desecrates Christ's face with a human love that contemplates this same face. It's as though one man's study repairs another man's sin. It's as though study has a role to play in redeeming the world. It's as though we need the virtue of studiousness to expand the kingdom of God in our own hearts and in creation.

If we really believed this, we would be willing to give God that most precious gift – our attention. ➷

1. Thomas Aquinas, *Summa Theologiae* II–II, q. 141, a. 2, ad 3. Cf. "Whether the Honest Is the Same as the Beautiful?" ST II–II, q. 145, a. 2.

2. Josef Pieper, *Happiness and Contemplation,* trans. R. & C. Winston (New York: Pantheon, 1958), 81.

3. Pieper, 75.

4. Ibid, 87.

5. ST II–II, q. 85, a. 2.

Bruce Herman, *François*, 2014

Ordinary Saints

The ordinary saints, the ones we know,
Our too-familiar family and friends,
When shall we see them? Who can truly show
Whilst still rough-hewn, the God who shapes our ends?
Who will unveil the presence, glimpse the gold
That is and always was our common ground,
Stretch out a finger, feel, along the fold
To find the flaw, to touch and search that wound
From which the light we never noticed fell
Into our lives? Remember how we turned
To look at them, and they looked back? That full-
-eyed love unselved us, and we turned around,
Unready for the wrench and reach of grace.
But one day we will see them face to face.

MALCOLM GUITE

Father Paolo
Dall'Oglio
in Nebek,
Syria, 2012

STEPHANIE SALDAÑA

An Impossible Hope

*Three men in Syria showed me
what Jesus looks like.*

 A SYRIAN PAINTER recently told me that we all have a map in our bodies, composed of the places we have lived, that we are constantly in the process of redrawing. A street from our childhood might be traversed by a train car in which we once fell in love. A garden from a year in London might yield, unexpectedly, a rose from the graveside of our grandmother. This map not only marks who we are but informs the way in which we encounter the world. The painter, a refugee originally from Damascus, was busily sketching the buildings of Istanbul, trying to move his map forward to the new country he now called home.

I am writing my map in the other direction. I am trying to remember who I am.

I lived in Syria more than a decade ago, and it was there that I met my husband. In a Syrian monastery perched up in the clouds, I rediscovered my faith. In Damascus I learned the Arabic that I still speak daily, and in a crumbling room in the Christian Quarter I began to write my first book. If my body is a map, Syria is the crossroads.

But I cannot go back. Now when I meet Syrians who have fled their country – living in refugee camps in Jordan, in the streets of Istanbul, in cafés in France – I ask them to tell me about the world they left behind. I sketch the details into the map of my body.

There were women who dried red peppers on the roofs of their houses in the old city of Aleppo. In Deir ez-Zor, a suspension bridge straddled the Euphrates River before it collapsed. A church in Homs was said to hold the belt of the Virgin Mary. In a garden in Daraa, we planted olive, lemon, orange, peach, and fig trees.

Every detail is a yes against the void. The 450,000 people dead. The estimated eleven million displaced.

There were two different kinds of apricot trees in the fields near Qaboun.

At the heart of my map is a monastery, and at the heart of that monastery is a man. To write this, I must remember him also and write him back into the map of my heart, which will not be easy. For he, too, has disappeared.

I WAS TWENTY-THREE the first time I journeyed to Deir Mar Musa, an ancient monastery high up on a cliff in Nebek, two hours north of Damascus. I was traveling through Syria for the first time, and rumor had it that one could visit a monastery in the desert that stood shining like a pearl, and that you could only get there by climbing a flight of 350 stairs. There was no need to tell anyone in advance that you were coming, and the monks and nuns who lived there would allow you

---

Stephanie Saldaña, a writer and native Texan, lives in Jerusalem with her husband. Her new book, A Country Between: Making a Home Where Both Sides of Jerusalem Collide, *appeared earlier this year (Sourcebooks).*

to stay as long as you wanted. The abbot was said to be an eccentric Italian, the community spoke Arabic, and the frescoes in the chapel were some of the most important in the entire Middle East.

I took a bus to Nebek and a smaller minivan into the desert. At some point the driver swerved onto a path that seemed to be headed nowhere, then eventually stopped. I looked up. The monastery was almost dreamlike, suspended. I began climbing, one step after another, for what must have been half an hour, ascending skywards amongst silence and the chiming of goat bells. At the top of the stairs, I met Father Paolo Dall'Oglio, a man as unlikely as the monastery itself.

Today, people often ask me what he was like, and the truth is that it is difficult to capture him in words. Father Paolo was less

a person than a force. He stood well over six feet tall, with wide shoulders and a deep baritone voice. He switched effortlessly between English, French, Arabic, and Italian, and he had taken up the habit of speaking like an old villager, in a dialect sprinkled with Arabic proverbs, like someone's grandfather. He wore plastic house sandals under his monastic robe. He liked eggs for breakfast. He was always trying to quit smoking.

He was a Roman and a Jesuit, both of these things through and through – passionate and always speaking with his hands, obsessed with the Jesuit notion of the *magis,* the idea that there is always more we can do for Christ. Deir Mar Musa, the monastery he founded in a difficult country and an even more inhospitable desert, was proof of that *magis.* He had first come to the monastery when he

The Mosaic Stories is a story-telling project that chronicles the endangered cultural heritage of the Middle East, especially Iraq and Syria. At a time when war and terror are dismembering traditions and communities, it profiles ordinary people in the region: musicians, cooks, soap makers, wedding dancers, members of religious communities, farmers, mothers. In the words of Stephanie Saldaña, who has helped spearhead the project: "It's the diverse people of the Middle East – not just its historic architecture – that is the region's most precious heritage." *mosaicstories.org*

was a student of Arabic in Lebanon, in the middle of the Lebanese Civil War. It was 1982, and Christians and Muslims in Lebanon were killing one another. He traveled on retreat to a ruined monastery in the Syrian desert, where he spent the night sleeping beneath a ceiling of stars. He prayed and eventually had the vision that would determine the course of his life: one day he would return to the monastery and restore it out of the ruins, creating a monastic community dedicated to prayer, contemplation, and hospitality. Yet it would not be just any monastery. The monks and nuns who took their vows there would promise to live their lives in dialogue with Islam.

It was an impossible hope, made in the depths of a sectarian civil war.

By the time I arrived, some eighteen years later, Deir Mar Musa was up and running. The stunning medieval frescoes of the church had been restored. A small community of monks and nuns had formed, named Al-Khalil, after Abraham, the *khalil* or special friend of God in the Quran, the common father of Muslims, Christians, and Jews.

I met Father Paolo again in 2001, as a journalist profiling the monastery after 9/11. After I diligently questioned him he turned the interview on me. I began to cry. This was the moment he became not an abbot in the desert but my spiritual father. Three years later I moved to Syria to study Arabic, and Father Paolo became a regular fixture in my life as I traveled out to the monastery on weekends and eventually completed the Spiritual Exercises of Saint Ignatius of Loyola – a month of silence and directed retreat – under his guidance. When I climbed the stairs, he was often waiting in the courtyard, not for me but for whomever happened to be climbing the stairs. Later I would come to understand that, for him, everything depended on those

encounters. For Father Paolo, those who would visit the monastery were tied up in his destiny. God sent them there.

Perhaps that was what unsettled so many of us who climbed those stairs, from all over the world: his insistence that this meeting was not an accident. Why did we come? Why did God bring us to the deserts of Syria? What does God desire for us to do in the world? He was never shy in asking the question.

It was in those years that Father Paolo taught me the theology of the sacred encounter. He believed that we must be changed by our meetings: with humans, with books, with religious traditions, with teachers living and dead. Meetings were our encounters with Christ himself, who came to us in a body. For this reason, Father Paolo's love of Christ was made manifest in his love of other things seemingly unrelated: his passionate love of the Quran, which he read often and quoted regularly, to both Muslims and Christians; the Islamic writings of mystics such as al-Hallaj; and the Arabic language itself, which he was so devoted to that he often corrected Syrians who mispronounced words during the readings of the Mass. He was attached to Louis Massignon, the great French Catholic scholar of Islam, as well as Massignon's friend Charles de Foucauld, the founder of the Little Brothers of Jesus, who had lived the last part of his life among the Muslims of Algeria. He was also deeply influenced by Gandhi and the writings of Simone Weil. Father Paolo once told me that all of us live in a chain of human beings, both living and dead, and our souls speak to one another.

He was an abbot, but he referred to himself

> For Father Paolo, those who would visit the monastery were tied up in his destiny. God sent them there.

most often as a monk. He was also a scholar, amassing a library in the desert that contained books in several languages on Eastern monasticism, Islamic mysticism, and philosophy. If you wanted to make him happy, you could arrive at the monastery with a chicken for the kitchen or a book for the library.

He spoke to me in English. He burst to life when Italian visitors arrived and he could converse in his mother tongue. He wrote in French. He prayed in Arabic. Every year, he fasted during Ramadan.

In short, he was a complicated man.

 N THE AYAT AN-NUR, the Verse of Light, the Quran speaks of God's light being like "a niche, within which is a lamp; the lamp is within glass; the glass is as if it were a pearly [white] star lit from [the oil of] a blessed olive tree, neither of the east nor of the west, whose oil would almost glow even if untouched by fire." Father Paolo once told me that he wondered if that "light" was the light that early monks lit in the desert.

The monastery of Mar Musa was as much for Muslims as it was for Christians, and Father Paolo would often declare that he was in love with Jesus, but also with Islam. In private conversations, he referred to his relationship with Islam as akin to marriage. He tried to express this love in the tiniest of details, things that would go mostly unnoticed by others but which spoke to a consuming desire to make Muslims feel that the monastery was their home. He left the wall in the chapel facing Mecca free of icons, in case Muslims wished to pray inside. He explained the frescoes of the church in Quranic terms when Muslims came to visit, so that Abraham became the Prophet Abraham. We all took off our shoes when we entered the chapel, as in a mosque. Even the

opening prayer every evening, when we sang out *nur ala nur,* or "light upon light," over and over again, resonated not only with the gospel, where Jesus is the "light of the world," but with the Quran's Verse of Light, where "Allah is the light of the heavens and the earth."

Every year, thousands of Muslims visited the monastery, and from the courtyard we could look down and watch them climbing the stairs from the valley below. Families would ascend on Friday afternoons after their picnics in the valley. Sheikhs would climb the stairs. Sufis would ascend to perform their chants. At lunch, the tables filled with young Christians chatting amicably with women in headscarves.

For Father Paolo, these meetings were not unlike those meetings in the Bible when the angels appeared as strangers and those receiving them were almost universally afraid. Many of the most significant moments in the text rely on welcoming an angel. The angels appearing to Abraham had special resonance for a community named in his honor, but it was the Annunciation, the angel Gabriel appearing to Mary, that I most vividly remember Father Paolo discussing.

We were at the point in the Spiritual Exercises when the angel appears to Mary. Mary says yes. This yes, mouthed in the face of uncertainty, allowed God to become incarnate. And so, Father Paolo believed, it is with us. Each time that we meet the Other and overcome our fear, each time we have the courage to say yes to the mysterious Stranger, who in the Middle East often comes as a Muslim guest, then the incarnation happens again. God appears among us in this love, this companionship, this meeting. Father Paolo had little patience for words such as "tolerance" to describe the interaction between Christians and Muslims. He was after something much more profound: a world in which we *need* one another to be complete,

Father Frans van der Lugt in the besieged area of Homs in January 2014, urging fellow residents to be patient despite severe shortages of food and medicine

a world in which we cannot live without one another because our encounter with the divine depends upon this destined meeting. Father Paolo was not interested in mere coexistence. He was interested in miracles.

I F YOU ZOOMED OUT from that map in my body, you would see that Mar Musa was part of a larger constellation of bodies dedicated to what might have seemed impossible in other countries: Christians and Muslims living together, bound up in one another's lives. To be a Christian in Syria during that time was to be able to participate in a remarkable church, where Christian priests were presiding over flocks of Christians and Muslims alike. Outside the nearby city of Homs, there was a farm called Al-Ard, a center run by the Dutch Jesuit priest Frans van der Lugt, who had lived in Syria for nearly fifty

years and who, like Father Paolo, was fluent in Arabic. He took care of children with disabilities, Muslim and Christian alike, and young Syrians would visit the center to volunteer and spend time with him and the residents. He led Zen meditation classes; I have a photograph of him, in his late sixties, standing on a simple straw mat with his hands in the air, leading Syrians in stretching exercises.

Father Frans was very different from Father Paolo. He was thin, unassuming, and balding, with gray hair and a kind face. He devoted himself to the children in his care. His theology was bound up in a profound sense of our common humanity, something I would think of as less Abrahamic and more Adamic. He became famous for his annual walks during which Muslims and Christians would trek together through Syria for days, befriending one another and falling in love with the

Father Jacques Mourad, 2017

landscape of their country as they struggled to keep up with this remarkable elderly man who led them. When they lagged, he encouraged them: *"Lil Iman! Go forth!"*

Finally, the third priest: Father Jacques Mourad, who had founded the community of Mar Musa with Father Paolo, helped to build and was now leading the church of Mar Elian in Al-Qaryatayn, one hundred kilometers north of Mar Musa on the road to Palmyra. Father Jacques was the only native Syrian of the three. He had a sweetness and quiet dignity about him and an incredibly beautiful singing voice. We loved it when he would visit Mar Musa and sing in the Syriac language during the Mass. In Al-Qaryatayn, a village that was home to both Christians and Muslims, he was well known for his deep relationship with Muslims as well as his devotion to his Christian faithful. But unlike Father Paolo, who was prone to grand statements, and Father Frans, who could walk across a country, Father Jacques quietly went about his work, loving his neighbors and never letting anyone claim that he was extraordinary.

History would write about these three men separately, but they were part of a single world. Father Paolo, Father Frans, and Father Jacques were constantly crossing paths, as were the young people who loved them. These young people at Mar Musa were also often in Al-Qaryatayn or Al-Ard, forming overlapping circles. It was a unique moment, less than eight years after the Catholic monks of Tibhirine had been martyred in Algeria. Dom Christian de Chergé, Tibhirine's French abbot, had formed a dialogue group with Muslims and had studied the Quran and developed a deep love of Islam, describing his love for Algeria and Islam as that of "a body and a soul." During the Algerian Civil War, the monks at the monastery had decided to remain in the country with their Muslim neighbors, an act of solidarity that cost them their lives.

FATHER PAOLO AND I held a conversation that we returned to each time we spoke. It concerned his idea that our deepest happiness was possible only on the cross, and began one day when he quoted

Plough Quarterly • *Summer 2017*

Simone Weil, who had once said: "When I think of Christ on the cross, I commit the sin of envy."

I accused him of making an idol out of suffering; he accused me of making an idol out of happiness. The conversation began in 2004, and would continue for the next nine years.

When Father Paolo flew to France to officiate at my wedding, during the sermon he brought up the cross again. It was an odd statement to make during a wedding, but he insisted on it. Love is only real if it is faithful on the cross. Marriage will inevitably have struggles, but we are called to love in the midst of them.

Over the years, he would bring it up repeatedly, this belief in redemption through the cross. I came to understand that his life choices could not be understood merely through his love of Islam but that they had to be paired somehow with his desire to be faithful to the redemption of the cross. He had decided to build a monastery in a desert, to enter into one of the world's most difficult places and to love there. In time, I came to think of his theology as simple: "the theology of fidelity," or, as I liked to call it, "the theology of staying put." We never abandon those we love.

HEN THE Syrian Civil War broke out in 2011, it quickly enveloped the world I have described, with protests soon centering on Homs, a Muslim city with a large Christian population. Father Paolo criticized the government openly, urging UN intervention. He was finally exiled from Syria in June of 2012.

In an interview with National Public Radio he said, "It would be better for me to be dead with the martyrs of this country than to go away in exile. I have offered my life for the future of this country, and I wish to stay in full solidarity with them, so I will come back."

Exile was perhaps the cruelest punishment for a man whose theology was based on fidelity. I spoke to him many times in the months that followed. I will always remember the last time, in July of 2013, when he called to tell me that he was traveling back to Syria after all. He had already snuck into the country before, and he had called me before that trip also, but this time felt different. I did not know when he was going. I did not know why. He wanted to speak, one last time, about love on the cross.

That morning, I had happened to read an interview in *The Paris Review* with the Polish poet Czesław Miłosz, who had also spoken of Simone Weil. Miłosz had noted that what drew him to her was her recognition of the reality of evil in the world. And yet she had also written about grace, the size of a mustard seed. "The little grain of mustard seed is really the kingdom of God, grace, and goodness," Miłosz explained, "small when compared with the evil in the world."

When Father Paolo asked me again about what I thought about choosing to suffer on the cross, I answered that Simone Weil's love of the cross could only make sense in light of this "mustard seed of grace." In a world in which there can be more evil than good, the point cannot be to defeat evil by conventional means. We will be overpowered, often outnumbered. We can overcome only through grace. Fidelity to the cross can only mean our willingness to go to difficult places, carrying that seed, and to believe that grace is transformative.

> Love and happiness, all of life itself, is possible on the cross, for it is here that redemption happens.

Of course, I asked him not to go. He told me that he had to. So I told him to carry that mustard seed of grace, to the darkest place in the world.

On July 29, 2013, Father Paolo went to meet with members of what would later be known as the Islamic State near Raqqa, hoping to negotiate the release of hostages. He has not been heard from since. We have not stopped waiting for him.

In the meantime Homs was under siege and the inhabitants were starving. Father Frans van der Lugt, now seventy-five years old, left Al-Ard and moved into the Jesuit residence in Homs's Old City. Refusing to leave his flock even as the fighting continued, he climbed onto his bike and rode through checkpoints, passing out bread.

The tomb of Father Frans in the Old City of Homs is visited by both Muslims and Christians.

When there was no bread, he starved with his neighbors, subsisting on olives and a broth of weeds. Eventually the siege ended, but some of the families did not leave and so he stayed with them. On April 7, 2014, a gunman knocked on the door and shot him to death.

Father Jacques Mourad continued on despite the increasing danger, using the aid money he received from church organizations to help the Muslim and Christian families in al-Qaryatayn, many of whom had fled from other areas. He negotiated for the village to be a zone safe from fighting, so that villagers would be protected. But in May of 2015, just days after they took Palmyra, ISIS militants kidnapped him and transferred him to a prison in Raqqa. The monastery of Mar Elian was razed to the ground. He was brought back to al-Qaryatayn and put under house arrest.

Eventually, no doubt with the help of local Muslims, he escaped.

WHEN I SET OUT to write this, I wanted to write about "impossible hope." But when I started writing, all I could think about were these men: Father Paolo, Father Frans, and Father Jacques.

Of course, Father Paolo was proven right in the end. Love and happiness, all of life itself, is possible on the cross, for it is here that redemption happens. The three of them chose to remain faithful to their flocks, not because they idolized suffering but because they knew that this was, oddly, choosing life. It was choosing love. It was believing in grace the size of a mustard seed, stronger than everything, even death.

The tomb of Father Frans in the Old City of Homs is visited by Muslims and Christians. A center for refugees in Lebanon has been dedicated in his name. This year, a group of Syrians now exiled in Europe who knew Father Frans started an annual walk in his memory.

Father Jacques is alive and well, serving as a priest in a monastery in Iraqi Kurdistan that welcomes Christian refugees who have fled from the Nineveh Plains.

Against all odds, the monastery of Mar Musa continues, perched high on a cliff at that strategic spot between Aleppo, Homs, and Damascus, between Iraq and Lebanon, in the heart of the cross. The community of Al-Khalil has remained faithful throughout the war. Recently, one of the monks of the community, Jihad Youssef, posted a picture of the mountains around the monastery, green and full of flowers in bloom.

He wrote: "Who would believe that this is the desert?" ⭢

Press, 2013

In These Surreal Times

Detecting Fake Reality with Paweł Kuczyński

SHANA BURLESON

He can't change the world, he says, but is "just the chronicler of our times." Artist Paweł Kuczyński was born in 1976 in communist-ruled Szczecin, Poland, just two months after widespread, violent protests rocked the country, opening the doors to organized opposition of the country's communist regime. During his early childhood, resistance groups sprang up throughout Poland, publishing clandestine

Shana Burleson is an editor at Plough.

Faces, 2013

Dinner, 2016

newspapers, establishing trade unions, holding secret university classes, and denouncing human rights violations.

The 1978 election of Pope John Paul II, formerly the Polish archbishop of Kraków, focused and united Poles; the new pope subtly encouraged resistance to the regime by encouraging the formation of an "alternative Poland" of social organizations independent of the communist regime. Kuczyński was five years old when martial law was imposed nationwide, leading to the imprisonment and mistreatment of thousands of Polish civilians in a violent crackdown that aimed to demoralize workers' unions and sap the will of members of the resistance.

But something else happened instead. In 1982, playful graffiti representing dwarves started appearing on walls where anti-communist slogans had been painted over by city governments. It was the beginning of a new phase of protest. The so-called

Love, Mind, and Phone, 2017

Orange Alternative was a student movement that focused on absurdist art as a means of dissent. From painted dwarves to public gatherings, the movement brought to the Polish anti-communist underground a sense of play, of humor, of the carnivalesque – and it lasted until the Berlin Wall fell in 1989. Two years later, in October 1991, Poland held its

first free parliamentary elections since the 1920s. Kuczyński was fifteen.

After secondary school, Kuczyński, who had always enjoyed drawing, specialized in graphics at the Academy of Fine Arts in Poznań. He painted portraits at parties, copied paintings of the masters, and painted apartment interiors. Then, in 2004, a friend

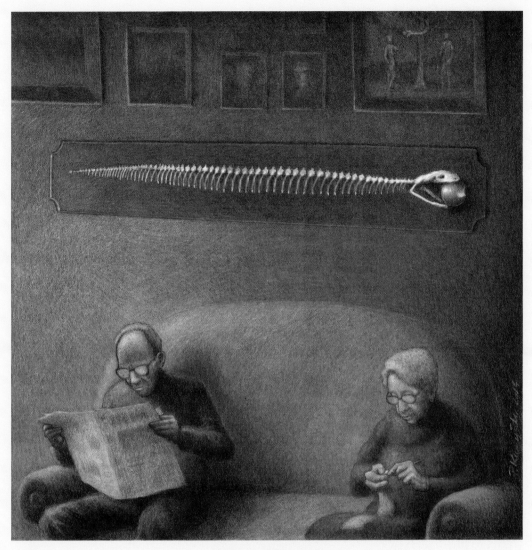

Adam and Eve, 2014

encouraged him to enter a cartoon competition. He drew his first satirical illustration and was hooked. Today, his thought-provoking art is recognized worldwide; his work has received over one hundred and thirty awards.

Kuczyński says he draws inspiration from his peers and colleagues as well as from the work of the old masters. He loves the theatrical lighting of Caravaggio's paintings, and often plays with light and shadows in his own works to create heightened drama.

As for subject matter, Kuczyński says that he doesn't have to look far – today's "absurd realities" offer plenty of material. Memories of the political uproar during his childhood motivate him to confront the apathy he sees

Money, 2007

Drone, 2014

in today's young people despite the troubling issues they face. Combining humor with frustration over Poland's political situation and global issues such as poverty, war, and racial division, he uses visual metaphors to bring out uncomfortable truths.

He has focused in particular on the way that our addiction to technology – and especially to social media – deforms human relationships and disrupts the inner life. His work shows a fierce commitment to the importance of that space in each of us that totalitarian regimes like the communism of his childhood had sought to colonize.

He's been called a surrealist. But Kuczyński demurs. He is, he says, "a realistic illustrator . . . of our surreal times." ⤏

Leon Dabo, *Silver Light, Hudson River*, 1911

Singing God's Grandeur

The All-or-Nothing Life of Gerard Manley Hopkins

DANA GIOIA

GERARD MANLEY HOPKINS is a singular figure in English-language literature. No other poet has achieved such major impact with so small a body of writing. His mature work consists of only forty-nine poems – none of which he saw published in his lifetime. Even when one adds the two dozen early poems written at Oxford and various fragments found in notebooks after his death, his literary oeuvre is meager in size, even for a writer who died in his forties.

Yet Hopkins occupies a disproportionally large and influential place in literary history. Invisible in his own lifetime, he now stands

as a major poetic innovator who, like Walt Whitman and Emily Dickinson, prefigured the Modernist revolution. A Victorian by chronology, Hopkins belongs by sensibility to the twentieth century – an impression strengthened by the odd fact that his poetry was not published until 1918, twenty-nine years after his death. This posthumous legacy changed the course of modern poetry by influencing some of the leading poets, including W. H. Auden, Dylan Thomas, Robert Lowell, John Berryman, Geoffrey Hill, and Seamus Heaney.

As W. H. Gardner and N. H. MacKenzie observed in the fourth edition of *The Poems*

Dana Gioia, the Poet Laureate of California, is the author of several books of essays and poetry, including most recently 99 Poems: New and Selected *(Graywolf, 2016).*

of Gerard Manley Hopkins (1970), "The steady growth and consolidation of the fame of Gerard Manley Hopkins has now reached a point from which, it would seem, there can be no permanent regression." There is a mixture of relief and wonder in their statement. No one would have predicted the poet's exalted position when the first edition was published, not even its editor, Robert Bridges, who spent much of his introduction apologizing for the poet's eccentricities and obscurities. Hopkins currently ranks as one of the most frequently reprinted poets in English. According to William Harmon's statistical survey of existing anthologies and textbooks, *The Top 500 Poems* (1992), Hopkins stood in seventh place among English-language poets – surpassed only by Shakespeare, Donne, Blake, Dickinson, Yeats, and Wordsworth (all prolific and longer-lived writers). His poetry is universally taught and has inspired a mountain of scholarly commentary. Despite the difficulty of his style, he is also popular among students.

Hopkins is one of the great Christian poets of the modern era. His verse is profoundly, indeed almost totally, religious in subject and nature. A devout and orthodox convert to Catholicism who became a Jesuit priest, he considered poetry a spiritual distraction unless it could serve the faith. This quality makes his popularity in our increasingly secular and anti-religious age seem paradoxical. Yet the devotional nature of his work may actually be responsible for his continuing readership. Hopkins's passionate faith may provide something not easily found elsewhere on the current curriculum – serious and disciplined Christian spirituality.

The history of English poetry is inextricably linked to Christianity. As Donald Davie commented in his introduction to *The New Oxford Book of Christian Verse* (1981), "Through most

of the centuries when English verse has been written, virtually all of the writers of that verse quite properly and earnestly regarded themselves as Christian." Not all poetry was explicitly religious, but Christian beliefs and perspectives shaped its imaginative and moral vision. The tradition of explicitly religious poetry, however, was both huge and continuous. Starting with Chaucer, Langland, and the anonymous medieval authors of *The Pearl* and *Sir Gawain and the Green Knight,* religious poetry flourishes for half a millennium. The tradition continues robustly through Donne, Herbert, Vaughan, Traherne, Cowper, Milton, Blake, Wordsworth, Tennyson, both Brownings, and Christina Rossetti – as well as the hymnodists Watts, Cowper, and Wesley. Then in the middle of the Victorian era it founders. Matthew Arnold's melancholy masterpiece of anguished Victorian agnosticism, "Stanzas from the Grande Chartreuse" (1855) exemplifies the crisis of faith. Entering the ancient Alpine monastery, Arnold contrasts the millennium of faith it represents with his own unsatisfying rationalism. Arnold articulates his intellectual and existential dilemma: "Wandering between two worlds, one dead, / The other powerless to be born."

Not coincidentally, it was during that moment of growing religious skepticism and spiritual anxiety that Hopkins appeared to transform and renew the tradition of Christian poetry. Consequently, he occupies a strangely influential position in the history of English-language Christian poetry. His audaciously original style not only swept away the soft and sentimental conventions of nineteenth-century religious verse, it also provided a vehicle strong enough to communicate the

> *Hopkins swept away the soft and sentimental conventions of nineteenth-century religious verse.*

God's Grandeur

The world is charged with the grandeur of God.
    It will flame out, like shining from shook foil;
    It gathers to a greatness, like the ooze of oil
Crushed. Why do men then now not reck his rod?
Generations have trod, have trod, have trod;
    And all is seared with trade; bleared, smeared with toil;
    And wears man's smudge and shares man's smell: the soil
Is bare now, nor can foot feel, being shod.

And for all this, nature is never spent;
    There lives the dearest freshness deep down things;
And though the last lights off the black West went
    Oh, morning, at the brown brink eastward, springs –
Because the Holy Ghost over the bent
    World broods with warm breast and with ah! bright wings.

GERARD MANLEY HOPKINS

overwhelming power of his faith. His small body of work – hidden for years – provided most of the elements out of which modern Christian poetry would be born.

Peggy Ellsberg's *The Gospel in Gerard Manley Hopkins* focuses on the central mystery of the author's singularly odd career – how a talented minor Victorian poet suddenly emerged after seven years of silence as a convulsively original master of English verse. For Ellsberg, Hopkins's conversion to Catholicism was the catalytic force, intensified by Jesuit spiritual discipline and intense theological study. Hopkins's poetic formation, she contends, was inextricable from his priestly formation. It was no coincidence that the great explosion of his literary talent occurred as he approached ordination. His conversion had initiated an intellectual and imaginative transformation – initially invisible in the secret realms of his inner life – that produced a new poet embodied in the new priest. For both the man and the writer, the transformation was sacramental.

Although Holy Orders plays a critical role in the chronology of Hopkins's transformation, the connections between his Catholicism and creativity do not end there. The author's religious and imaginative conversion, Ellsberg demonstrates, depended on his vision of all the sacraments, especially the Eucharist. "For him," Ellsberg formulates persuasively, "a consecration made from human language reversed existential randomness and estrangement." Hopkins's belief in transubstantiation and real presence saved him from the painful theological doubts and sentimental spiritual hungers of his Anglican contemporaries; their crepuscular nostalgia and vague longing were replaced by his dazzling raptures of light-filled grace. A brave new world filled his senses with the sacramental energy of creation where every bird, tree, branch, and blossom trembled with divine immanence.

From the start, Hopkins's literary champions have been puzzled, skeptical, confused, or even hostile toward his conversion. Catholicism was seen, even by Robert Bridges, as an intellectual impediment that the poet's native genius somehow overcame, though not without liability. Or Hopkins's theology was a cerebral eccentricity that generated an equally eccentric literary style. Ellsberg refutes these condescending views of the poet and the Church. She pays a great poet the respect of taking his core beliefs seriously, not in the least because they have also been both the animating ideas of European civilization and the foundational dogmas of the Roman Catholic Church, which have inspired artists for two millennia.

The Gospel in Gerard Manley Hopkins combines scholarly accuracy with critical acumen. Ellsberg's extensive commentary on Hopkins's verse and prose texts both elucidates his thought and provides illuminating context for the poems. Meanwhile she sustains her larger argument on the spiritual development of the author as a model Christian life of consecration, contemplation, sacrifice, and indeed, sanctity. In restoring the focus on the centrality of Hopkins's faith, Ellsberg does not simply clarify the underlying unity of his life and work. She also restores a great poet and modern saint to us, his readers. ⇝

> *For Hopkins, every bird, tree, branch, and blossom trembled with God's immanence.*

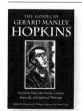

Taken from the foreword to a new Plough *book,* The Gospel in Gerard Manley Hopkins: Selections from His Poems, Letters, Journals, and Spiritual Writings, *ed. Margaret R. Ellsberg. Learn more at plough.com/hopkins.*

We
Cannot
Give
What
We
Do Not
Have
———
Time for
the
Benedict
Option?

The Great Catch Mosaic © 2001 John August Swanson / Eyekons. Courtesy of Concordia University Irvine

On March 16 of this year,

hundreds gathered at the Union League Club in midtown Manhattan for a public conversation about the future of Christianity in the West. The occasion was the launch of Rod Dreher's new book *The Benedict Option,* a *New York Times* bestseller dubbed by David Brooks as "the most discussed and most important religious book of the decade." The event, co-hosted by *Plough, First Things,* and the *American Conservative,* brought together a varied group for a lively panel discussion.

In the face of an increasingly hostile culture, how should Christians approach participation in public life? What kinds of communities can foster true discipleship? How can we raise our children to follow Jesus? These are some of the questions raised by the book and addressed by the panelists.

Dreher began by laying out the ideas in the book and addressing common criticisms. Other panelists responded, including Ross Douthat of the *New York Times*, Jacqueline C. Rivers of the Seymour Institute for Black Church and Policy Studies, and Randall Gauger, a Bruderhof bishop. Here, we present excerpts from that conversation. (Michael Wear, a former Obama White House staffer, was also a panelist; his remarks, plus a full video of the event, appear in our digital edition.)

Media organizations from *The Federalist* to the *New Yorker* covered the event. And the conversation hasn't stopped: see the item titled "City and Kingdom New York" on page 7 to learn about a new initiative co-sponsored by *Plough* that aims to continue to address these crucial issues.

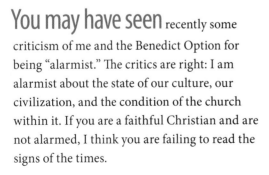

Rod Dreher | *It is time for the Benedict Option.*

You may have seen

recently some criticism of me and the Benedict Option for being "alarmist." The critics are right: I am alarmist about the state of our culture, our civilization, and the condition of the church within it. If you are a faithful Christian and are not alarmed, I think you are failing to read the signs of the times.

I do not claim that *the* world is coming to an end. No man knows the day or the hour. What I am claiming is that *a* world is coming to an end, and that if Christians don't take radical action now, the faith that made Western civilization will not survive for long into its post-Christian phase.

A few years ago, a noted public intellectual said that "it is obligatory to compare today's situation with the decline of the Roman Empire. In its final days, Rome still functioned as a great historical framework, but in practice its vital energy had been depleted." The intellectual went on to lament the collapse of the spiritual forces that sustain us.

That public intellectual was Joseph Ratzinger, Pope Benedict XVI. When the heir of a global throne that has been in existence for nearly two thousand years says that the West is facing its greatest spiritual crisis since the fall of the Roman Empire, attention must be paid.

What are the signs of the times, then? After all, the West is living in a time of unprecedented peace and prosperity, though I hardly need to point out the sense of mounting political crisis throughout our civilization. But signs of our spiritual depletion are impossible to deny – and if we are spiritually depleted, and morally exhausted, our peace and prosperity will not last long.

I won't recite a litany of statistics, but I do want to focus on a few that are of particular interest to Christians:

1. The Christian faith is flat on its back in secular Europe. The United States has long been thought a counterexample to the secularization thesis. That is no longer tenable. Writing last year in the *American Journal of Sociology,* scholars David Voas and Mark Chaves say the data now show that the United States is on the same downward path to disbelief pioneered by our European cousins.

2. According to data from the Pew Research Center, one in three 18–29-year-olds have put religion aside, if they ever picked it up in the first place.

3. Those younger Americans who remain affiliated in some capacity with churches have been formed by a pseudo-religion that resembles Christianity in name only. Notre Dame sociologist Christian Smith and his colleagues call this "Moralistic Therapeutic Deism" (MTD). MTD uses the language and conceptual vocabulary of historical, biblical Christianity, but in fact it teaches a malleable, feel-good, Jesus-light philosophy perfectly suited to a consumerist, individualistic, post-Christian society that worships the self. Smith and his research colleagues found that MTD is the de facto religion of most young Americans today.

4. In findings published in 2011, Smith found that among 18–23-year-old Christians surveyed, only 40 percent said that their personal moral beliefs were grounded in the Bible or some other religious sensibility.

5. An astonishing 61 percent of these so-called emerging adults said they have no moral problem at all with materialism and consumerism. An added 30 percent expressed some qualms but figured it was not worth worrying about. In this view, say Smith and his team, "all that society is, apparently, is a collection of autonomous individuals out to enjoy life."

"America has lived a long time off its thin Christian veneer, partly necessitated by the Cold War," Christian Smith told me in an interview. "That is all finally being stripped away by the combination of mass-consumer capitalism and liberal individualism."

The Marxist sociologist Zygmunt Bauman coined a phrase that perfectly captures the revolutionary spirit of our time and place: "liquid modernity."

Rod Dreher is a senior editor at the American Conservative *and the author most recently of* The Benedict Option: A Strategy for Christians in a Post-Christian Nation (*Sentinel, 2017*).
▶ *Watch the full video of the March 16, 2017 event at* plough.com/benop.

Modernity, as we know, is characterized by a conscious break with the authority of the past and its institutions. For Bauman, "solid modernity" describes the first phase of modernity, in which the pace of change had quickened, but was still slow enough for people to adjust. Things still seemed, well, solid.

But now we have moved into liquid modernity, a time in which the pace of change is so rapid that nothing – no new institutions, no new habits or customs – has time to solidify. In liquid modernity, Bauman said, the most successful person is the one who has no allegiances beyond himself and his self-interest. He can change loyalties and beliefs at will, to suit his own preferences. There is no solid ground anymore.

From a Christian perspective, I liken liquid modernity to the Great Flood of the Bible. All the familiar landmarks of our faith are being submerged and swept away. The flood cannot be turned back. The best we can do is construct arks in which we can ride out and, by God's grace, make it across the dark sea of time to a future when we find dry land again and can start the rebuilding, reseeding, and renewal of the earth.

What is the Benedict Option,

and what does it have to do with this dire scenario I paint? The term comes from the famous final paragraph of Alasdair MacIntyre's 1981 book, *After Virtue*. In that book, the philosopher explained how Enlightenment modernity overthrew the old source of moral order, the one rooted in Christianity and classical philosophy, but could not produce an authoritative replacement for it. The West has been unraveling for some time now, and is reaching a point of reckoning.

Liberalism is not sufficient to do the necessary work of binding society together and giving its members purpose.

In his book's conclusion, MacIntyre too compared our present time to Rome's collapse, although he indicated that our wealth obscures our inner fragility from our eyes. In post-imperial times, he said, some men and women of virtue quit trying to shore up the existing social order and instead focused on building new forms of community within which they could live out their moral traditions amid civilization's ruins. MacIntyre famously said that today, we await "a new – and doubtless very different – Saint Benedict."

Benedict of Nursia is known today as the founder of Western monasticism and as a patron saint of Europe. He was born in the year 480, four years after the last Roman emperor abdicated, and was sent as a pious young man down to the city of Rome to complete his education. What he saw there disgusted him. Benedict lit out for the forest to pray and fast and seek God's will for his life. Eventually he founded twelve monasteries governed by a kind of monastic constitution called *The Rule of Saint Benedict*.

The Rule is a thin, plain pamphlet for the running of a monastery, which he called a "school for the Lord's service." It is not a book of spiritual secrets. It is a book that sets out an order for living, for the sake of training monastics in the spiritual life. You would never guess from reading it that this little book played a key role in saving Western civilization.

After Benedict died, monasticism

exploded. Monks moved all over barbarian-ruled Europe. They brought the faith to unchurched people. They taught them how to pray, but also how to grow and make things – skills that had been lost in Rome's collapse. In their rituals and in their libraries, the monks kept alive the cultural memory of Christian Rome. Because the monks took a vow of stability – a sacred promise to remain in the monastery where they took their vows until the end of their lives – peasants gathered around the monasteries as citadels of light and order in a very dark and chaotic time.

In this way, the Benedictine monasteries were arks carrying the faith across the stormy waters that obliterated Roman civilization. It all happened not because Saint Benedict of Nursia set out to "make Rome great again," but because he sought to figure out how to best serve the Lord in community during a terrible crisis. Everything else followed from that.

In *The Benedict Option,* I write about my visits to the Benedictine monastery in Norcia, as Saint Benedict's hometown is known today. I interviewed the monks about how their core values and practices can be applied to everyday Christian life outside the monastery. Prayer, work, hospitality, asceticism, stability, community – in Benedictine daily life, all these things work together in balance to lead the monks towards a sense of life-giving order, suffused by a sense of the sacredness of life.

Father Cassian Folsom, who was at the time the prior, or leader, of the Norcia monastery, told me that the monastery, with its life of Christ-focused prayer, is a sign of contradiction to the modern world:

> The guardrails have disappeared, and the world risks careening off a cliff, but we are so captured by the lights and motion of modern life that we don't recognize the danger. The forces of dissolution from popular culture are too great for individuals or families to resist on their own. We need to embed ourselves in stable communities of faith.

What does this look like for ordinary Christians – Catholic and otherwise – who are called to live in the world? Does the Benedict Option call for Christians to head for the hills and build high walls to keep the impurity of the world at bay?

Not at all! We have to evangelize, or we fail the great commission. We have to serve our neighbors, or we fail to serve our Lord. Put all thoughts of total withdrawal out of your mind. That is not what the Benedict Option calls for.

But it does call for a *strategic separation* from the everyday world. What do I mean by that? I mean that we have to erect some walls, so to speak, between ourselves and the world for the sake of our own spiritual formation in discipleship. In this hedonistic, post-Christian society, the dissipating force of outside culture is overwhelming. We cannot expect to go out into it and keep our candle lit any more than we could leave the church building in a gale-force wind and do so.

Here's the paradox of the Benedict Option: if the church is going to be the blessing for the world that God means for it to be, then it is going to have to spend more time away from the world deepening its commitment to God, to scripture, to tradition, and to each other. We cannot give to the world what we do not have. We should engage with the world, but not at the expense of our fidelity and our sense of ourselves as a people set apart. We must somehow walk a path between the Christian fundamentalists who reject *everything* about the world and the accomodationists who love the world so much that they rationalize idol-worship for the sake of preserving their privileges. "Engaging the culture" must never

"If we don't change our way of living, we will not survive as the church."
Rod Dreher

become an excuse to burn a pinch of incense to Caesar. Winsomeness must never be a veil concealing our cowardice from ourselves.

There must have been something about the daily lives of Shadrach, Meshach, and Abednego in Babylon that trained them spiritually so that when they were put to the ultimate test, they passed. It must be that way with us, too. We are failing at this today, and failing badly. The numbers I cited earlier tell a tale of Christian infidelity. If we don't change our way of living, we will not survive as the church. We will be assimilated. There is no middle way.

> ## "The greater problem right now is the erosion of authentic Christianity by individualism, hedonism, and consumerism."
>
> Rod Dreher

Do I worry about persecution? To an extent, yes. You cannot talk to law professors, doctors, educators, and others who follow the religious liberty debate and remain sanguine about the future. Pastors and parents who do not prepare those under their authority for that kind of future are failing in their duty. But as I see it, the greater problem right now is the steady erosion of authentic Christianity by the relentlessness of individualism, hedonism, and consumerism. And we also must face the fact that in some quarters on the right, we are seeing the rise of an ungodly racism.

If we are going to stay true to our faith, we are going to have to listen to voices from outside the here and now – authoritative voices from the Christian past, especially the premodern era. How else are we going to be able to tell the difference between those who speak comforting lies that we want to hear and those who, like Jeremiah, preach the prophetic word of God? We must beware of religious leaders who are content to be chaplains to the contemporary cultural order. That way is death.

Marco Sermarini is an Italian Catholic layman and community leader who is one of the new and very different Saint Benedicts of our time. When I visited his thriving, joyfully orthodox Catholic community in Italy, I asked him how they did it. He said to me: "We invented nothing. We discovered nothing. We are only rediscovering a tradition that was locked away inside an old box. We had forgotten."

Modernity is a time of forced forgetting. The Benedict Option is, in a sense, a project of preserving the memory of what it is to be Christian. Hope is memory plus desire. If we remember who we are and desire to make those memories live again, we have every reason to hope. But we cannot ignore the warning that Father Cassian of Norcia gave me when I visited. The monk told me that if Christian families and communities in the West do not do some form of the Benedict Option, "they're not going to make it." ■

Ross Douthat | *Dreher is right even if he's wrong.*

I feel like I have been on panels having arguments about the Benedict Option for as long as I have been a journalist. So it is wonderful to actually have a book to tell people to go buy and argue about and disagree with.

I should say that usually when I have been on those panels, there is a debate like the one that Rod alluded to in his remarks, where somebody says, "Well, this is all very well and good, but you surely can't be arguing that we should just head for the hills." Then Rod tears his beard and rips off his glasses and says, "I'm not saying we should head for the hills!" And it goes on from there.

I won't play the role of that interlocutor. But I'll go half way and say that my take on *The Benedict Option* is that Rod is right even if he is wrong.

By which I mean that – you know, this was a very, very gloomy portrait that Rod just painted of the future of Christianity in the West and particularly in the United States. Those of you who occasionally read our parish newspaper know that I am not noted for my sunny optimism. Yet even I occasionally, listening to Rod, reading his blog, and reading the pages of this very fine book, do sometimes creak my eyebrow up a little bit and say, "Well, is it really so bad as all that?"

I think there are some reasons to be doubtful. I generally have less confidence about all predictions about the future than I did since the startling rise of Donald Trump over the last eighteen months, including especially my own predictions about politics; but extending also to extrapolations of present trends into the future. In that sense, I think we are at a place in the story of American Christianity where we see through a glass darkly. We can't know for certain if what we are seeing when we look at the trends that Rod describes is a collapse just of cultural Christianity; a collapse in people's identification with a faith that they never really held to begin with. That sort of collapse would have some important effects on the life of the church, but it wouldn't lead to, let's say,

a Netherlands- or Belgium-style collapse for American Christianity (meaning no offense to the five remaining Christians in the Netherlands and Belgium).

But we don't know if that is the scenario we are looking at or if we are looking at something more complete and sweepingly disastrous, as Rod suggests. And there are a lot of things that make our situation and our future even more unknowable than usual. For instance, we are about ten or fifteen or twenty years, depending on how you time it, into the great internet experiment, which may only be accelerating. Rod writes a great deal about that in his book – very eloquently and, I think, persuasively. But there is at bottom a sort of unknowability about what the internet is doing to social life, what it is doing to religious life, what it is doing to childhood and adolescence. All these are things that will become clear to us over the next twenty or thirty or two hundred years, but aren't clear right now.

The same is true of the interaction between religious life and our unexpectedly unsettled politics in the West. The same is true of the interaction between religious life and advances in various other forms of technology: biotechnology and so on.

So there is a long list of reasons why I'm just not certain if Rod is right about where we are going overall. But I also don't think it necessarily matters that much, because I think where we are right now is clearly a place where many of the things he calls for, the cultural practices that he advocates, are necessary and useful and

> ## "We should be trying to build (or rebuild) resilient communities."
> Ross Douthat

Ross Douthat is the author of several books including Bad Religion: How We Became a Nation of Heretics *(Free Press, 2012). He is a columnist for the* New York Times.

important, no matter what happens in ten or twenty or thirty years.

We wouldn't be at this moment in our politics and our common culture if we weren't living in a more fragmented, individualistic, and post-communitarian landscape than almost any generation in American history. We are living in an increasingly post-Tocquevillian United States, you might say – in the sense that many of the things that Tocqueville described as distinctive about the United States that he visited in the early nineteenth century and that remained distinctive about this country down until the 1960s and arguably even until the 1990s and 2000s – a basic resilience of local community, local religious life; a denominational competition as a spur to bottom-up social order – those things that we have taken for granted are fragmenting and falling apart.

In that landscape, that situation, we should be trying to build (or rebuild) resilient communities – resilient Christian communities, resilient religious communities, resilient communities, period. (Even if you are part of the Society for Secular Humanism you can have your own version of the Benedict Option if you really want it – or maybe not. We can argue about that later.) Building resilient communities may not be *the* answer; there may be other things we need, but it is an incredibly important answer to the challenges of our time.

> ## "We don't exactly have a surplus of monks in the United States."
> Ross Douthat

And that includes even some of the touch of extremism in Rod's advocacy, which I think should hit home for people.

Here I'll mildly break *New York Times* rules and talk about one of my fellow columnists' columns. David Brooks, my dear friend and Rod's, wrote a column about Rod's book where he said something to the effect of, "It sure seems like there are a lot of monks in this book." One response that I have to that is the one that I wrote in my own column, which was basically to say, "Well, yes; but the message of Rod's book isn't that everyone should become a monk. It's that everyone, from where they are, perhaps, should take one step in a more monastic direction." And I do think that is one important way to read *The Benedict Option*. To say, "Don't assume that you need to personally revolutionize the liturgy in your parish. Don't assume that you need to pull your kids out of whatever school they are in immediately and build an organic farm and so on. Assume that you need to take one step for now, one step towards a more Benedictine way of life."

That's one response. But I'll finish by saying the thing that occurred to me after writing that column, which was that we don't exactly have a surplus of monks in the United States, and it wouldn't necessarily be the worst thing if lots of people read Rod's book, which is indeed filled with monks, and said, "Hey, maybe there's a vocation there for me to think about."

But my wife has forbidden me to become a monk, so that more extreme step is for someone else. ∎

This is a particularly telling time in Western culture – a time when Christian values that were once widely accepted and enshrined in law in Western nations are increasingly vanishing from the public square and being replaced by radical individualism. The need for Christians to resist the seductions of today's culture is real and just as pressing as the need to remain engaged as a public witness to the gospel. The time is ripe for a more robust and dedicated Christianity, similar to the practice of the early Christians, the original Benedict Option. However, the crisis in Western culture must not be conflated with a crisis of Christianity, which is thriving in the global south, particularly in Africa. Indeed, it is essential, even as we discuss the need to resist Western culture, to acknowledge the strength of global Christianity and the black church here in the United States in order not to alienate the fastest-growing segment of the population: non-white people.

Western Christians must seriously reconsider the original Benedict Option, as described in Acts 2:42–47:

> They devoted themselves to the apostles' teaching and to fellowship, to the breaking of bread and to prayer. Everyone was filled with awe at the many wonders and signs performed by the apostles. All the believers were together and had everything in common. They sold their property and possessions to give to anyone who had need. Every day they continued to meet together in the temple courts. They broke bread in their homes and ate together with glad and sincere hearts, praising God and enjoying the favor of all people. And the Lord added to their number daily those who were being saved.

This is really the model for Christian life; we should be doing the things that are outlined here: devotion to prayer, scripture, and fellowship. Our churches have fallen far short of this, instead practicing "cultural Christianity" and becoming very weak as a result. I remember being bewildered at the Harvard Christian Fellowship as an undergraduate. I was a new Christian, and I thought that Christianity was supposed to turn your life upside down, reorder your priorities, and transform you. With these young people, it was warm milk and cookies. Just as Dreher describes in his book, the students were concerned with consumerism, getting a Harvard degree, and going on to be extremely comfortable financially.

One aspect of Acts 2 that I take very seriously is the promise of signs and wonders. In the Pentecostal Church, the belief that God has the power to heal and to work miracles, even in the twenty-first century, is one we take seriously, although this belief is rare in today's churches.

There's another verse in Acts we fall short on: "The believers were together and shared everything in common." Do we care for each other that way? Instead, we lead atomized

> "The time is ripe for a more robust and dedicated Christianity."
> Jacqueline C. Rivers

Jacqueline C. Rivers, PhD, is director of the Seymour Institute for Black Church and Policy Studies.

lives, separated from each other. We don't know our neighbors, and often church is just a matter of watching the clock: "When is he going to end? It's one hour and one minute. Church is supposed to be over in an hour." But there isn't time for fellowship, for connection, for investing in each other's lives, for caring for each other radically, as these people did, because they met every day. If anybody was in need, they were ready to sell what they had in order to take care of one another. That is the original Benedict Option. Dreher's book should be celebrated because it holds up the biblical model for Christianity, which has been overlooked.

But I am concerned that in the book, there is a conflation of Christianity with Western culture. Dreher writes of Christianity's retreating into the Benedict Option to survive a cultural cataclysm as it did in the Dark Ages in Europe. He presents communal living as a ship to take us across the dark waters to a more friendly time when Christian culture can resurface. But the crisis he describes is really limited to the West. Christianity was born in the Middle Eastern milieu. Of all the books of the Bible, only Luke and Acts were written by a European. Many of the foundational developments in Christianity actually took place in North Africa and moved from there into Europe: think of early church fathers like Origen, Ignatius, and Athanasius. Christianity will survive the fall of the West, because it's God's work, not the work of the West. And today, according to a 2011 report from the Pew Research Center, Christianity is truly a global religion: "In 1910 about two-thirds of the world's Christians lived in Europe. Today one in every four Christians

lives in Sub-Saharan Africa, and about one in eight is found in Asia and the Pacific." In sub-Saharan Africa, the Christian population climbed from 9 percent in 1910 to 63 percent in 2010.

One strategy we might explore is to draw on the dynamic, Holy Spirit–filled strength of the church in Africa and in South America to launch a revival in our creaky white churches here in the United States. This revival is important because many millennials have been alienated by misreading the claim to religious freedom as an excuse for discrimination. When we should have been championing the cause of people who feel same-sex attraction and often lead divided and painful lives, we condemned them. As a result, millennials reject us and view the church as a source of the problem. But we black people are the ones in this country who have suffered the most grievous discrimination and who continue to be harmed by structural racism and mass incarceration. It was our faith that inspired our ancestors to lead the civil rights movement. If we stand up and talk about religious freedom, we have a level of credibility that is unparalleled in the rest of the church, because too often millennials and others associate the white churches with racism rather than with championing the cause of the poor.

When my husband, Eugene Rivers, and I were undergraduates at Harvard, Eberhard Arnold's writings powerfully turned us on to this original Benedict Option, especially his books *The Early Christians* and *Why We Live in Community*. My husband was struck by the authentically radical character of the Bruderhof understanding of Christian faith and practice and their sincerity in actually carrying it out. Several of us traveled from Harvard to

the Deer Spring Bruderhof in Connecticut to see the community in action. We were struck by it, but we weren't ready to retreat from our vision of living in the city to serve the urban poor. Returning to inner-city Boston, we tried to build community, drawing on the model of shared work that we saw at the Bruderhof.

I am really grateful for the role that the Bruderhof played in shaping our spiritual lives as we faced the challenge of building a community among the poor. It's even harder to resist the consumerist culture if you have never had it, and everybody else has. We faced some of those difficulties, as well as the question of how to educate the next generation, which Dreher also raises in his book.

Dreher is right that much of the Christianity that is practiced in the West is compromised and reflects the values and aspirations of secular culture. Western Christians must be prepared to make substantial sacrifices to resist the culture. But hasn't that always been true? One area where the need is especially strong is in resisting the subtle forms of racism that ignore the vibrant fidelity of thriving African churches. Similarly, to dismiss the vital role of the black church in the United States in repudiating charges of discrimination that are being leveled against the exercise of religious freedom is to alienate an important segment of the population. Authors such as Dreher need not speak for the global south or the black church, but they must acknowledge the critical role they play in Christianity. It is essential to the credibility of our analysis. ■

Randall Gauger | *It's not an "option," but a calling.*

It is encouraging that many people are joining this important conversation about how we as Christians can more faithfully follow Jesus. At the same time, it seems that the most frequent reaction to Rod Dreher's ideas – a yowl of protest about "withdrawal" in favor of "engagement" – misses the main point he is making and is the reverse of my own experience about living out my faith.

So my first point is this: building a communal church along the lines Rod suggests allows Christians to engage more, and more meaningfully, with our fellow human beings. Assimilation to the ways of the world is as dangerous as Jesus warns us – Dreher is right

in pointing to this. But the stronger the center, the more daring the outreach can be.

My own life is an illustration of this. For the past thirty years, my wife, Linda, and I have been members of the Bruderhof, a Christian communal church in the Anabaptist tradition that is almost one hundred years old, in which we share all things in common in the spirit of the first church in Jerusalem. I believe that we have been able to engage both more deeply and more broadly with society than if we had remained as a private family.

Linda and I are both farm kids from the Midwest who grew up in what would be called dysfunctional homes. Our families were

A Minnesota native, Randall Gauger is a bishop in the Bruderhof community and lives in southwest Pennsylvania.

nominally Christian: Lutheran in my case and Catholic in Linda's. But faith in Jesus meant nothing to us – by our mid-twenties we were on the road to conventional middle-class life: we had a house, two kids, two cars, and two TVs. But we were unhappy. Something was missing.

Through a Bible study we came to faith in Jesus. Later, as we read in the Book of Acts, we were struck by the witness of the early church. The realization that they shared everything, sold their possessions, and ate and worshipped together came as a shock to us. The Book of Acts tells that this was the result of a movement of repentance and the coming of the Holy Spirit. This excited us and drove us to seek a life of community. So we started living in community with a few other families. This lasted for about five challenging and exciting years as we continued searching.

Then we ran across the writings of Eberhard Arnold, the founder of the Bruderhof. His depth of understanding of living for Jesus and the kingdom answered many of our questions. In his book *Why We Live in Community* he writes: "Community life for us is an inescapable must. . . . We must live in community because we are compelled by the same Spirit that has led to community time and time again since the days of biblical prophecy and early Christianity." Those words thrill me today as much as thirty years ago when I first read them. So we came to the Bruderhof in 1987.

> "The stronger the church's center, the more daring its outreach can be."
> Randall Gauger

Our life since then has been one of intense engagement with every imaginable segment of society. I'll describe some of this, not to sing the praises of the Bruderhof – we have plenty of weaknesses – but to show what community life makes possible.

Actually, for the past seventeen years, Linda and I lived at a Bruderhof community in rural Australia – the ultimate "withdrawal," you might think. But it wasn't.

In the first place, there was simple neighborly contact with the locals: barbecues, Christmas carol sings, invitations to each other's homes and churches. Community members also pitched in with babysitting, home care for elderly shut-ins, and home repairs. This extended to my work as a police chaplain with the New South Wales police force. Other community members serve on local fire brigades and with emergency medical services.

As part of stewardship of the earth, we collaborated with local farmers in sustainable agriculture techniques, which have already made a measurable difference to our area.

Our community also partners with local charities as well as organizations like World Vision and Save the Children – we support them financially and our young people volunteer in crisis situations.

We hosted thousands of guests from all over Southeast Asia – everyone from itinerant hipsters to federal politicians to the local Aboriginal community, leading to an unforgettable moment when one of their elders blessed the site of a house that we built last year.

Linda and I visited other church communities all over Australia and in Thailand and South Korea.

Would we have done as much as a solitary nuclear family? I doubt it. There certainly are individuals who achieve this level of connectivity just by force of personality. But this brings me to my second point. Society, and especially Christian society, needs to create space for the weak and broken as well as those with extraordinary talents.

Only in a communal church can the old and the very young, hurting military veterans, the disabled, the mentally ill, ex-addicts, ex-felons, or the simply annoying find a place where they can be healed and, what's more, contribute. I share a common meal every day with brothers and sisters that answer to each of these descriptions. Those who preach "engagement" often fail to think how we as Christians can actually bear each other's burdens – whether economic, medical, or emotional – outside of strong communities. Where is the love in "engaging" the world if we don't have time for an emotionally fragile neighbor? Pope Francis gets something right in speaking of the church as a "field hospital."

And on to my third point: building strong communal churches actually isn't an "option" – it's our *calling* as disciples. My constructive criticism of Dreher, actually, is that he isn't taking his own proposal seriously enough.

The Rule of Saint Benedict is a wonderful, wise, and important document. But why stop at Benedict when you can go back to the original source of Christianity? Christians living in full community is how the church began. It's the only way I know where Jesus' teachings in the Sermon on the Mount become a practical reality. And the early church was far more radical than anything Dreher has so far proposed. The early Christians turned the world upside down, sharing all things in common (actually, Saint Benedict has some strong words to say against private property!); evangelizing the whole known world; refusing to participate in violence of any kind, including self-defense, military service, abortion, or the death penalty; modeling a new ethic of sexuality and family life that honored the equal dignity before God of both men and women; and revolutionizing

Greco-Roman society. Nobody can accuse the early Christians of withdrawal!

This is not a life for the faint-hearted. It requires an all-or-nothing, full-time, lifetime commitment – what T. S. Eliot called "the condition of complete simplicity / costing not less than everything." It won't be enough to apply a few aspects of *The Rule of Saint Benedict* that happen to dovetail pleasingly with a private, middle-class American lifestyle. How many of us are like the rich young man who couldn't accept Jesus' invitation because he wasn't able to part with his possessions? Yet the early church did not come into existence by means of moral efforts or legalistic rules, but because of the joy of following Jesus.

Linda and I would live in church community whether society were going to pieces or not. The life I live is a calling from Jesus and the best way I have found to follow him. And this way is not just for a few traditional Christians, or the most radical among us – it's actually the good news and the new life that Jesus wants for all people. As Rod puts it in the conclusion of his book, fittingly titled "The Benedict Decision:" "We find others like us and build communities, schools for the service of the Lord. We do this not to save the world but for no other reason than that we love him and know that we need a community and an ordered way of life to serve him fully." ⤳

> "My constructive criticism of Dreher is that he isn't taking his own proposal seriously enough."
> Randall Gauger

Editors' Picks

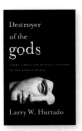

Destroyer of the Gods
Larry W. Hurtado
(Baylor University Press)

The early Christians' contemporaries branded them irrational, simple, wicked, hateful, obstinate, and antisocial. The new religion was so different from the pagan religions of its day that it wasn't even recognized as one; Christians were called atheists. Most notably, adherents were actually expected to behave differently, and unlike Judaism, the movement transgressed ethnic and social boundaries. This scholarly yet readable survey tells the unlikely story of the movement's explosive growth, often through the words of its critics and detractors.

Today, many of the beliefs and practices that were distinctive back then are commonplace. Who believes in dozens of gods anymore? But modern Christians have much to learn from our foreparents' spunk and distinctiveness. There are more than a few new idols and false gods to be toppled.

12 Ways Your Phone Is Changing You
Tony Reinke
(Crossway)

The smartphone, which didn't even exist a few years ago, has become an indispensible tool in your work to serve Christ and lead others to him – at least, that's what many believe. But you have likely also abused it, and if you haven't worried about how this powerful technology is shaping your habits, your mind, your relationships, and your spiritual life, you probably ought to.

In this incisive, thoroughly researched, and thoughtful book, Reinke, a Christian journalist and self-professed phone addict, uncovers more pits and snares than you may care to acknowledge (distraction, fear of missing out, craving approval, becoming harsher, secret vices, etc.). But such self-examination is essential if we are to live healthy and balanced lives in the digital age. Reinke lets us draw our own conclusions, but the implication is clear: If we don't approach this intentionally and take some practical steps to resist, we will get washed downstream.

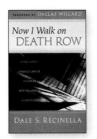

Now I Walk on Death Row
Dale S. Recinella
(Chosen)

A Wall Street finance lawyer ends up on death row. He calls it the work of the Holy Spirit (and a raw oyster, but that's another story). In this reverse Horatio Alger tale, Recinella, his wife Susan, and their children decide Jesus meant what he said, but when they announce that they are ready to leave behind the good life to serve Jesus full-time, their bishop tells them they are over-zealous. Recinella recounts the adventures that follow, including stints here at the Bruderhof and at other communities, which finally lead him to his life calling: ministering to the men on Florida's death row. He accompanies many to their death and even witnesses a botched execution.

Recinella, a one-time *Plough* editor who recently stopped by our offices, has also written a definitive theological work on capital punishment, *The Biblical Truth about America's Death Penalty,* and a Catholic guide to prison ministry, *When We Visit Jesus in Prison.* ⟋ *The Editors*

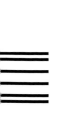

BUSINESS REPLY MAIL
FIRST–CLASS MAIL   PERMIT NO. 332   CONGERS, NY

POSTAGE WILL BE PAID BY ADDRESSEE

PLOUGH QUARTERLY
PO BOX 345
CONGERS NY 10920–9895

SPECIAL OFFER: 55% OFF!

Stories, ideas, and culture to inspire faith and action

Plough Quarterly

1 year (4 issues) just $18!

(Includes FREE access to *Plough*'s digital version and archives)

☐ PAYMENT ENCLOSED ☐ BILL ME

Name _____

Address _____

City _____ State _____ Zip _____

Email (for e-newsletter and updates) _____

www.plough.com/subspecial

Canadian orders add $8 per year; $16 for other foreign. Please allow 4–6 weeks for delivery of your first issue. Plough Quarterly is $40 per year by single copy. For faster service call **1-800-521-8011** or go to www.plough.com/subspecial.

BLN2017

(Continued from page 80)

Nonviolent Coordinating Committee (SNCC) to recruit local blacks to register to vote. She knew that she was risking her home, her job, her life. But "the only thing they could do to me was kill me," she said, "and it seemed they'd been trying to do that a little bit at a time ever since I could remember."

Although eighteen prospective registrants traveled to the county courthouse, only Hamer and one companion were permitted to take the literacy test, which they "failed." (Examinees were required to interpret sections of the Mississippi constitution; examiners routinely applied far more rigorous standards to blacks than to whites.) In the bus on the way back, the group was discouraged, afraid of consequences awaiting them. Hamer began to sing, and others joined in. "This little light of mine," they sang, "I'm gonna let it shine. . . ." The song would become her signature.

Back home, Hamer found W. D. Marlow, the owner of the plantation where she and her husband had worked for eighteen years, in a rage. He demanded that she withdraw her registration. She refused, quitting her job on the spot. She and the children left the plantation that same night. Hamer kept organizing – and singing. By 1963, she had become recognized as a significant leader in the Mississippi civil rights struggle.

On June 9, 1963, on their way back from a citizen training workshop, Hamer and several other civil rights workers were arrested. In jail, they were tortured and sexually violated. Hamer, beaten brutally, suffered permanent eye and kidney damage.

It was the story of this ordeal she told at the 1964 Democratic National Convention, where she and others were attempting to secure representation for the new Mississippi Freedom Democratic Party, which included both black and white delegates. She raised her voice before a national audience, and at least at that moment, America listened. Her televized testimony was so electrifying – and so potentially damaging to Southern Democrats – that President Johnson hastily called a press conference, as he remarked to his aides, to "get that illiterate woman off the air." Although efforts to secure delegate seats at the convention failed, Congress passed the Voting Rights Act within the next year, ensuring federal oversight of elections, and Hamer was seated as a Mississippi delegate at the 1968 Democratic presidential nominating convention.

Fannie Lou Hamer

"We are fighting these people because we love them and we're the only thing that can save them."

Meanwhile, Hamer started focusing on economic power. Freedom Farm was born out of her conviction that food and land were keys to freedom for those in the chains of poverty – and that these keys should be held by black and white neighbors together. "We are not fighting against these people because we hate them," she said, "but we are fighting these people because we love them and we're the only thing that can save them now."

Fannie Lou Hamer died of cancer and heart failure on March 14, 1977. She was fifty-nine years old. To the end, she would not compromise either on justice or on mercy, speaking for her people but insisting on the dignity of every person, fighting for freedom – and for reconciliation and forgiveness. "A city that's set on a hill cannot be hid," she said. "And I don't mind my light shining; I don't hide that I'm fighting for freedom, because Christ died to set us free." ➤

▶ *Listen to Fannie Lou Hamer singing "Precious Lord" to Charlie Evers, brother of the murdered civil rights worker Medgar Evers, at* plough.com/hamer.

Photograph by Ken Thompson

Fannie Lou Hamer

JASON LANDSEL

IN 1969, Mrs. Fannie Lou Hamer bought forty acres of farmland in the Mississippi Delta and started the Freedom Farm Cooperative of Sunflower County. The co-op was Hamer's version of direct action, meant to create both economic power and community solidarity among local families. And it was worked, and owned, by blacks and whites together.

Fifteen hundred families joined, putting in work in exchange for a share of the harvest. They could also borrow a pregnant pig, keeping the piglets and returning the mother to the farm's so-called pig bank. The results: food for families who had struggled to afford it, a hedge against the uncertainties of the collapsing sharecropping economy, and a sense of independence.

"All the qualifications that you have to have to become part of the co-op is you have to be poor," Hamer said. That was something she knew about. The youngest of twenty children, Hamer was born into a sharecropping family in 1917, one hundred years ago this October. She started picking cotton at age six and had to quit school at age twelve, working adult hours on the plantation to help put food on the table. Still eager to learn, she attended Bible classes at the local church and read everything she could get her hands on.

The injustice around her ate at her heart. She knew the local waterways contained the murdered remains of many like herself. She knew that her family, having struggled to save enough to buy mules and a pair of cows, had been thrown back into poverty when a resentful white neighbor poisoned their livestock.

She once asked her mother why she wasn't white. Her mother, who illegally packed a 9mm Luger in the fields to keep her kids safe, told her that she must respect herself for who she was. Her mother also taught her to sing: songs of freedom, of trust in God.

Hamer retained her mother's fighting spirit – and commitment to forgiveness. "Ain't no such a thing as I can hate anybody and hope to see God's face," she'd later say. She loved the words of Paul quoted in Acts 17:26, remarking:

> It's long past time for the churches to wake up. Jesus wasn't talking about black people, or about white people. . . . There's no difference in people, for . . . Paul says, "God hath made of one blood all nations of men for to dwell on all the face of the earth." That means that whether we're white, black, red, yellow, or polka dot, we're made from the same blood.

When she was twenty-seven, she married Perry Hamer. Unable to have children, the couple took in two little girls and would later adopt two more. Then, in 1961, Mrs. Hamer went in for a surgery and woke up to find that she'd been given a hysterectomy. This was common at the time: a "eugenic" measure, meant to prevent black women from "breeding." This experience colored her lifelong opposition to abortion, which was fundamentally driven by her understanding of the sacredness of human life. "Legal abortion is legal murder," she would say, claiming that it "amounts to genocide" against African Americans.

Her "Mississippi appendectomy" (she coined the term) finally spurred Hamer to action. She began working with the Student

(Continued on preceding page)

Jason Landsel is the artist for Plough's *"Forerunners" series, including the painting opposite.*